Modern Art Movements

1 Piet Mondrian *The Red Tree* 1909-10. 27½ × 39 in. (70 × 99 cm.). Gemeentemuseum, The Hague

2 Piet Mondrian *The Grey Tree* 1911. 30¾ × 41½ in. (78.5 × 107.5 cm.). Gemeentemuseum, The Hague. S. B. Slijper Collection

3 Piet Mondrian *The Flowering Apple Tree* about 1912. 30¾ × 41¾ in. (78.5 × 106 cm.). Gemeentemuseum, The Hague

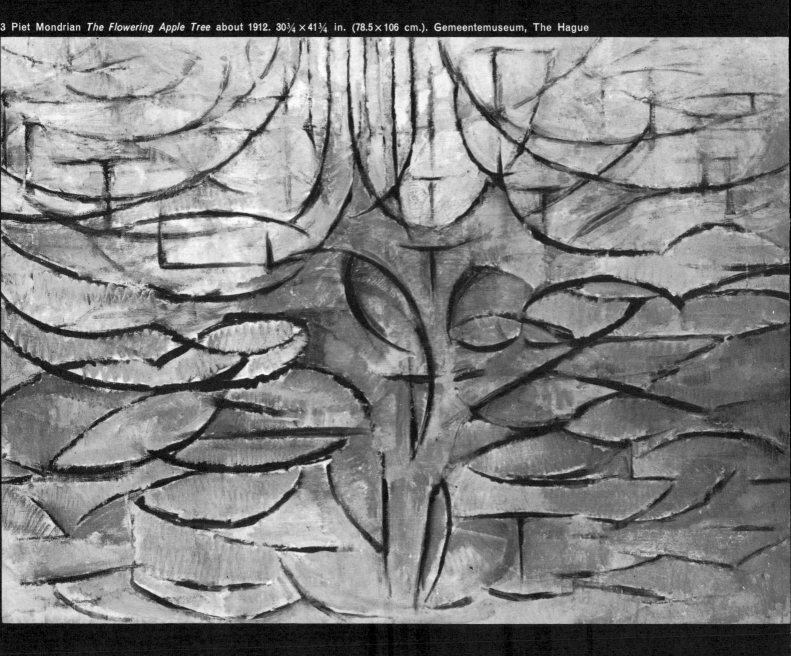

Trewin Copplestone

Modern Art
Movements

The Colour Library of Art
Paul Hamlyn·London

ACKNOWLEDGMENTS

The paintings in this volume are reproduced by kind permission of the following collections, galleries and museums to which they belong: Acheson Collection, New York (Plate 19); Bayerische Staatsgemäldesammlungen, Munich (Plates 28, 33); City Art Gallery, Leeds (Plate 4); City of Leicester Art Gallery (Plate 31); Galerie Beyeler, Basle (Plate 7); Galerie Chalette, New York (Plate 46); Gemeentemuseum, 's-Gravenhage (Figures 1, 3); Gemeentemuseum, 's-Gravenhage. S. B. Slipjer Collection (Figure 2); George F. Goodyear and the Buffalo Fine Arts Academy, N. Y. (Plate 38); Peggy Guggenheim Collection, Venice (Plate 53); Solomon R. Guggenheim Museum, New York (Plate 26); Lady Hulton Collection, London (Plate 15); Riccardo Jucker Collection, Milan (Plates 35, 36); Kunsthalle, Hamburg (Plates 21, 22, 25); Kunstmuseum, Basle (Plates 14, 27, 30); Kunstmuseum, Basle. Sonia Delaunay Donation (Plate 40); Musée National d'Art Moderne, Paris (Plates 12, 17); Musée de L'Annonciade, Saint-Tropez (Plate 8); Museum of Modern Art, New York (Plates 9, 11, 13, 34, 37, 39, 43); Museum von der Heydt der Stadt Wuppertal (Plate 29); Nasjonalgalleriet, Oslo (Plate 20); National Gallery of Art, Washington D. C. Chester Dale Collection (Plate 6); Vicomtesse de Noailles Collection, Paris (Plate 48); Nolde-Museum, Seebüll (Plate 24); Sir Roland Penrose Collection, London (Plate 50); Philadelphia Museum of Art. Louise and Walter Arensberg Collection (Plates 16, 18, 49); Rijksmuseum Kröller-Müller, Otterlo (Plates 41, 45); Alfred Roth Collection, Zurich (Plate 42); Royal Museum of Fine Arts, Copenhagen (Plates 1, 2); Madame G. C Signac Collection Paris (Plate 3); Stedelijk Museum, Amsterdam (Plates 23, 44, 54); Trustees of the Tate Gallery, London (Plates 5, 10, 32, 47); Trustees of the Tate Gallery, London. On loan from the Edward James Foundation (Plate 51). The following photographs were supplied by Colorphoto Hans Hinz, Basle (Plates 14, 27, 30, 40); Michael Holford, London (Plate 53); André Held - Joseph P. Ziolo, Paris (Plate 7, 8). Plates 1, 2, 3, 7, 8, 9, 10, 11, 12, 13, 17, 32, 47, 48, 53 are © by S.P.A.D.E.M., Paris 1967. Plates 4, 5, 6, 14, 15, 16, 18, 19, 25, 26, 39, 50, 51, 54 are © by A.D.A.G.P., Paris 1967.

First Published 1962
Revised Edition 1967

Published by Paul Hamlyn Limited
Drury House · Russell Street · London WC2
© Paul Hamlyn Ltd 1962
Printed in Italy by Officine Grafiche Arnoldo Mondadori, Verona

Contents

THE PLATES *All paintings reproduced are oil on canvas unless otherwise stated*

1 Henri Matisse. *Self-portrait.* 1906. 21 ³/₄ × 18 in. (54 × 46 cm.). Royal Museum of Fine Arts, Copenhagen

2 Henri Matisse. *The Green Stripe (Mme Matisse).* 1905. 15 ³/₄ × 12 ¹/₂ in. (40 × 32 cm.). Royal Museum of Fine Arts, Copenhagen

3 Henri Matisse. *Luxe, Calme et Volupté.* 1904-05. 37 × 46 in. (94 × 127 cm.). Madame G. C. Signac Collection, Paris

4 André Derain. *Pool of London.* 1906. 32 × 39 in. (81 × 99 cm.). Leeds City Art Gallery

5 André Derain. *Portrait of Matisse.* 1905. 18 ¹/₈ × 13 ³/₄ in. (46 × 35 cm.). Tate Gallery, London

6 Albert Marquet. *Le Pont-Neuf.* 1906. 19 ⁵/₈ × 24 in. (50 × 61 cm.). The National Gallery of Art, Washington, D.C. Chester Dale Collection

7 Raoul Dufy. *Promenade au Quai.* 1905. 18 × 21 ¹/₄ in. (46 × 54 cm.). Beyeler Gallery, Basle

8 Maurice Vlaminck. *Les Bâteaux-Lavoirs.* Chatou 1906. 52 ³/₄ × 20 in. (73 × 50 cm.). Musée de L'Annonciade, Saint-Tropez

9 Pablo Picasso. *Les Demoiselles d'Avignon.* Spring 1907. 96 × 92 in. (243.9 × 233.7 cm.). Collection, The Museum of Modern Art, New York. Acquired through the Lillie P. Bliss Bequest

10 Pablo Picasso. *Seated Woman (Nude).* 1909-10. 36 ¹/₄ × 28 ³/₄ in. (92 × 73 cm.). Tate Gallery, London

11 Pablo Picasso. *Ma Jolie (Woman with a Zither or a Guitar).* 1911-12. 39 ³/₈ × 25 ³/₄ in. (100 × 65,4 cm.). Collection, The Museum of Modern Art, New York. Acquired through the Lillie P. Bliss Bequest

12 Pablo Picasso. *The Violin.* 1914. 25 $^1/_2$ × 18 in. (65 × 46 cm.). Musée National d'Art Moderne, Paris

13 Pablo Picasso. *Three Musicians.* Summer 1921. 79 × 87 $^3/_4$ in. (200.7 × 229.9 cm.). Collection, The Museum of Modern Art, New York. Mrs Simon Guggenheim Fund

14 Georges Braque. *The Portuguese.* 1911. 45 $^7/_8$ × 32 $^1/_8$ in. (116 × 83 cm.). Kunstmuseum, Basle

15 Georges Braque. *Bottle, Glass and Pipe.* 1914. 19 $^1/_8$ × 25 $^1/_2$ in. (48 × 65 cm.). Lady Hulton Collection, London

16 Juan Gris. *Still Life in Front of an Open Window.* 1915. 45 $^3/_4$ × 35 in. (116 × 89 cm.). Philadephia Museum of Art. Louise and Walter Arensberg Collection

17 Fernand Léger. *The Wedding.* 1912. 101 × 81 $^1/_8$ in. (257 × 206 cm.). Musée National d'Art Moderne, Paris

18 Marcel Duchamp. *Nude Descending a Staircase.* 1912. 37 $^3/_4$ × 23 $^1/_2$ in. (96 × 60 cm.). Philadelphia Museum of Art. Louise and Walter Arensberg Collection

19 Jaques Villon. *Little Girl at the Piano.* 1912. 50 $^3/_4$ × 37 $^3/_4$ in. (129 × 96 cm.). Acheson Collection, New York

20 Edvard Munch. *The Dance of Life.* 1899-1900. 49 $^1/_4$ × 79 $^3/_4$ in. (125 × 202 cm.). Nasjonalgalleriet, Oslo

21 Ernst Ludwig Kirchner. *The Artist and Model.* 1907. 59 × 39 $^3/_8$ in. (150 × 100 cm.). Kunsthalle, Hamburg

22 Carl Schmitt-Rottluff. *Landscape, Loftus, Norway.* 1911. 34 $^1/_4$ × 37 $^3/_4$ in. (87 × 96 cm.). Kunsthalle, Hamburg

23 Max Pechstein. *The Harbour.* 1922. 31 $^1/_2$ × 39 $^1/_4$ in. (80 × 100 cm.). Stedelijk Museum, Amsterdam

24 Emil Nolde. *The Windmill.* 1924. 28 $^3/_4$ × 30 $^3/_4$ in. (73 × 78 cm.). Nolde Museum, Seebull

25 Wassily Kandinsky. *Arab Cemetery.* 1909. 28 $^1/_8$ × 38 $^5/_8$ in. (71 × 98 cm.). Kunsthalle, Hamburg

26 Wassily Kandinsky. *Black Lines.* 1913. 50 $^3/_8$ × 50 $^3/_8$ in. (128 × 128 cm.). Solomon R. Guggenheim Museum, New York

27 Franz Marc. *The Fate of Animals.* 1913. 76 $^3/_4$ × 105 $^1/_2$ in. (195 × 268 cm.). Kunstmuseum, Basle

28 Franz Marc. *Fighting Forms.* 1914. 35 $^7/_8$ × 51 $^5/_8$ in. (91 × 131 cm.). Bayerische Staatsgemäldesammlungen, Munich

29 Alexei von Jawlensky. *Peonies.* 1909. 40 $^1/_2$ × 30 in. (103 × 76 cm.). Museum Von der Heydt der Stadt, Wuppertal

30 Oscar Kokoschka. *The Tempest.* 1914. 71 $^3/_4$ × 86 $^3/_8$ in. (181 × 220 cm.). Kunstmuseum, Basle

31 Lyonel Feininger. *The Square.* 1916. 29 × 35 $^1/_2$ in. (74 × 90 cm.). City of Leicester Art Gallery, Leicester

32 Paul Klee. *Young Girl's Adventure.* 1922. Watercolour on paper. 17 $^1/_4$ × 12 $^5/_8$ in. (43 × 32 cm.). Tate Gallery, London

33 Max Beckmann. *Self Portrait.* 1914. 37 × 24 in. (94 × 61 cm.). Bayerische Staatsgemäldesammlungen, Munich

34 Umberto Boccioni. *The City Rises.* 1910. 78 $^1/_2$ × 118 $^1/_2$ in (199.3 × 301 cm.). Collection, The Museum of Modern Art, New York. Mrs Simon Guggenheim Fund

35 Umberto Boccioni. *Elasticity.* 1912. 39 $^3/_8$ × 39 $^3/_8$ in. (100 × 100 cm.). Riccardo Jucker Collection, Milan

36 Umberto Boccioni. *The Charge of the Lancers.* 1915. Tempera and pasted papers. 13 × 20 in. (34 × 51 cm.). Riccardo Jucker Collection, Milan

37 Giacomo Balla. *Speeding Automobile.* 1912. Oil on wood. 21 $^7/_8$ × 27 $^1/_8$ in. (55.6 × 68.9 cm.). Collection, The Museum of Modern Art, New York. Purchase

38 Giacomo Balla. *Dog on a Leash.* 1912. 35 $^5/_8$ × 43 $^1/_4$ in. (91 × 110 cm.). George F. Goodyear and the Buffalo Fine Arts Academy, N.Y.

39 Gino Severini. *Dynamic Hieroglyphic of the Bal Tabarin.* 1912. Oil on canvas with sequins. 63 $^5/_8$ × 61 $^1/_2$ in. (161.6 × 156.2 cm.). Collection, The Museum of Modern Art, New York. Acquired through the Lillie P. Bliss Bequest

40 Luigi Russolo. *Houses and Lights.* 1912. 39 $^3/_8$ × 39 $^3/_8$ in. (100 × 100 cm.). Kunstmuseum, Basle. Sonia Delaunay Donation

41 Piet Mondrian. *Composition with Colour Planes on White Ground.* 1917. 19 $^3/_8$ × 17 $^3/_8$ in. (49 × 44 cm.). Rijksmuseum Kröller-Müller, Otterlo

42 Piet Mondrian. *Composition.* 1930. 18 × 18 in. (46 × 46 cm.). Alfred Roth Collection, Zürich

43 Piet Mondrian. *Broadway Boogie Woogie.* 1942-43. 50 × 50 in. (127 × 127 cm.). Collection, The Museum of Modern Art, New York

44 Theo van Doesburg. *Counter Composition.* 1924. 39 $^1/_4$ × 39 $^1/_4$ in. (100 × 100 cm.). Stedelijk Museum, Amsterdam

45 Bart van der Leck. *Geometrical Composition.* 1917. 39 $^3/_4$ × 39 $^1/_4$ in. (101 × 100 cm.). Rijksmuseum Kröller-Müller, Otterlo

46 Cesar Domela. *Composition.* 1926. 31 $^3/_4$ × 20 in. (81 × 51 cm.). Galerie Chalette, New York

47 Max Ernst. *Of This Men Shall Know Nothing.* 1923. 31 $^5/_8$ × 21 $^1/_4$ in. (80 × 64 cm.). Tate Gallery, London

48 Max Ernst. *Monument to Birds.* 1927. 64 × 51 $^1/_4$ in. (162 × 130 cm.). Vicomtesse de Noailles Collection, Paris

49 Salvador Dali. *Premonition of Civil War.* 1936. 43 $^1/_4$ × 33 $^1/_8$ in. (110 × 83 cm.). Philadelphia Museum of Art. Louise and Walter Arensberg Collection

50 Joan Miró. *Maternity.* 1924. 36 $^1/_2$ × 28 $^1/_4$ in. (93 × 72 cm.). Sir Roland Penrose Collection, London

51 René Magritte. *Time Transfixed.* 1932. 60 × 48 in. (152 × 122 cm.). Tate Gallery, London. On loan by Mr Edward James

52 Kurt Schwitters. *Das Haarnabelbild (The Hair Navel).* 1920. Oil on board with painted relief of wood, cloth earthenware and hair. 35 $^3/_4$ × 28 $^1/_2$ in. (91 × 72.5 cm.). Lords Gallery, London

53 Giorgio de Chirico. *The Rose Tower.* 1913. 28 $^3/_4$ × 28 $^3/_8$ in. Peggy Guggenheim Collection, Venice

54 Marc Chagall. *Maternity.* 1913. 76 $^3/_8$ × 45 $^1/_4$ in. (194 × 115 cm.). Stedelijk Museum, Amsterdam

Introduction

'They provoke laughter and are altogether lamentable. They show the most profound ignorance of design, composition and colour. Children amusing themselves with paper and paints can do better.' This quotation from Ballu, a nineteenth-century professional critic, might well be taken as a generally held view of modern painting, but in fact it was written in 1877 about the paintings of Monet and Cézanne. There is nothing new in this sort of criticism, but we have learnt to treat it with some reserve, for experience has taught again and again that such violent antipathy usually turns out to have been misplaced. More often than not, in painting, it is directed at what is commonly described as the *avant-garde* and, as Clemenceau remarked in defence of the then reviled Impressionists, the future is always with the *avant-garde*.

As the reader will anticipate, this book is concerned with the work of such forward-looking artists and tries to show that such a judgment as that given above is as unwise in respect of the modern artist as it has proved to be for the Impressionists.

The whole of modern art is too broad a canvas for a short book of this kind, and only six important groups of painters found in Europe during the first three decades of this century are examined. This is not an inappropriate limitation, for much of the subsequent art of the century owes a great deal to the inspiration of Cubists, Futurists, Surrealists, etc. Too often, in fact, the importance and character of these individual and separate groups is thrown together in one incoherent amorphous mass and labelled 'modern art'. Some value, and not a little increase in appreciation, will probably follow from their disentanglement.

The above quotation probably expresses the bewilderment of many people today when they confront modern paintings. Thus before we consider the individual movements, we should take a closer look at the nature of modern art, how and why it differs from the art that went before, and what the modern artist is trying to do, although this may lead us into generalisations which can only broadly be true and may not help greatly in front of individual works. It will be as well to deal first with the process of artistic creation itself.

The 'quality' of a work of art depends upon the 'quality' of the artist who produces it. It is the result of his intelligence, his sensitivity to things that may stimulate him and his technical competence; these derive from his character, his understanding and his temperament. The particular form that the work takes arises from the direction in which his interests lead him and from his technical sympathy with one method of expression rather than another. This is true, I think, of all the arts, and the artist becomes a painter or a sculptor because the visible world and the materials of his craft — paint, colour, stone, volume — are the things that move him to express himself in art. A painter paints not because he wants to represent what he sees and is competent to do so, but because the visible world stimulates him to satisfy his deep urge to shape his understanding of life and nature. He paints because he cannot avoid it. It is, as a consequence, not an easy or time-passing activity but one which demands his whole concentration and his whole personality, one which may destroy his health and separate him from his fellows. It is apparent that not only talent but dedication is essential and if it is fair and accurate to regard the artist's life in this way, it is also fair that the work should have the serious and careful attention of the observer.

A work of art may be described as the sharing of experience. As such it stands on its own, divorced from everything — even from the man who produced it, although it may mean more to him than to anyone else. (It may not of course; since art is a cathartic activity, once the work is produced the artist may lose all interest in it — several artists, indeed, have been known to leave their paintings where they finished them.) The work, then, on its own stands as an object and actually comprehends what the artist has, from his experience, been able to put into it. His technical ability is what has enabled him to give the work the inspirational or emotive quality that it has. It is this quality that it may transmit to the observer.

The observer is the third part of a creative triangle. Any comment on a work of art is also a comment on the observer, and the participation of the observer in the creative act is the last stage in its effectiveness.

The artist is never in the last analysis, and in most cases in the first, concerned with the observer. This is true of all art at all times. He may anticipate the participation of the observer in his experiences and he may have produced the work at the instigation of others — the church, the state or the private patron of the Renaissance — but ultimately he is alone in the creative process. No artist will ever alter the work at the instigation of others if he is convinced of its completeness. Any changes he makes for others will be an admission of failure to realise his own inspiration completely or will be such as will not affect the nature of the work. When Velasquez allowed Philip IV to paint the Cross of St George on his breast — if he did — it was only because it did not affect the whole character of the picture. Whatever the level of the art, this remains true. But whilst the observer is irrelevant to the artistic activity he is nevertheless essential. Although it might be argued that a work of art, destroyed as soon as produced, being the complete expression of the artist and containing his 'qualities', is not diminished by not being seen, it is nonetheless true that in these circumstances art becomes a pointless activity except to the artist. Since I would suggest that art is a necessary aspect of human life its display is important.

But who is the observer? Is it the critic who professionally appreciates, is it the fellow artist who may understand the problems, is it the connoisseur, is it the patron or collector, is it the 'man in the street' or is it anyone who gives the work anything from a casual glance to a careful study? Of course in one sense it is all of these, but who among these establishes the quality of the work? Is the 'man in the street' to take the estimate of the critic as his yardstick, is the collector to take the man in the street as his adviser? Undoubtedly a hierarchy of quality in works of art has been established; how did this come about and on whose authority? Why should we speak of Rembrandt, Michelangelo or Velasquez with bated breath, and who has imposed Picasso, Kandinsky or Mondrian upon us? These questions are fair and pertinent, and it is not easy to answer them for the subject of 'appreciation' is very complex.

In a straight sense the observer is every individual who observes and he is, *must* be, the judge of quality. The only importance of a work of art is its importance to you. It is of no significance that others value it; it is your valuation that is significant and if you say that it is empty, spurious, specious, ugly, beautiful, elevating, imaginative, moving, then it is so. For others, of course, this is a comment on you, for the truth is that the observer himself is involved in the question of quality. His quality is as much at the bar as the painting's; uninformed or insensitive comment on anything reveals itself and is noted as such. The sensitivity, experience, receptiveness, character of the observer are involved and, as in every sphere of life, his quality determines the value of his estimate and the depth of his response. Comments on great works are as negligible or valuable as the response that evoked them. For this reason on the subject of art the observer's comments must be seen in the context of their quality and sensitivity.

What then does a sensitive observer experience when he confronts a work of art? A preliminary point of considerable importance should be made. The artist is a special creative spirit, special in the sense that he is creative and special in the sense that he confines his creativity to the form he adopts. As a specialist he is set apart and as a creative spirit he is, as history reveals, in a small minority. The observer shares in the creative act in that it discharges itself through him: what he experiences is part or all of the transmuted experience of the artist; how much this is will depend on his sensitivity and temperament and on the creative power of the artist.

The quality of both painter and observer will be the result of innumerable influences. Background, environment, heredity are obvious factors but there are others not so obvious though not less formative. Social attitudes, current conventions of thought, accidental associations, small events of great personal significance and the influence of other personalities are a vital and unique part of each individual's make-up. One must also include the unconscious responses, developed during growth; responses to colour, shape or line in combination are not the same for everyone — indeed, recent research has revealed that there is an extraordinary range of colour response in vision itself. Coincidental juxtapositions of colour and line may recall to the observer events in his personal life which may make them attractive or repulsive and lend them importance which is special to the individual. At the same time there are general or common responses to colours and shapes which, although not universally, will usually evoke similar responses from all observers. When we remember, as Maurice Denis has reminded us, that 'a painting, before it is a horse, a nude, or some sort of anecdote, is essentially a flat surface covered with colours assembled in a certain order', it becomes clear that the responses of the painter and observer to these alone are factors in any work of art. In fact the quality of the painter and of the observer is the whole personality of each, and art can accept nothing less.

From what has been said it follows that the creative intention of the artist and the response of the observer may not be identical. Even where the artist has completely realised his intention and the observer is unusually sensitive, the feeling that the painting evokes in the observer may be very different from the artist's inspiration. We may go further and say that two observers will never have identical responses. The communion between the work of art and the observer is as private and unique as that between the artist and his work.

This accepted, the appreciation of a work of art is a complex business deeply and inextricably involved with the cultural life of man. The artist is not just a copyist of nature's appearance; he is part of the fabric of society, an involuntary revelation of its character. He uses nature, the visible world, but his whole purpose is the interpretation of his personal — and necessarily limited — understanding.

Although he uses nature, this is not to say that his paintings must resemble nature. Indeed 'abstraction' is a device much used in art (and not only in modern art). It is therefore unfortunate that it should be so thoroughly misunderstood, and since it is so much a part of modern painting some examination of it is essential. To abstract has two general senses: to deduct or take away, and to summarise. In relation to modern art it partakes of something of both senses but predominantly of the first. It would probably be helpful to distinguish two general uses of the term.

In one use it describes paintings in which a particular subject — landscape, figure or still life — has been used as the basis for an arrangement and the shapes used have been taken from the subject and altered to coincide with the understanding of the painter. The stages and character of this process are clearly shown in the three illustrations of a tree by Mondrian. In the first (figure 1) the form of the tree and the way in which it is painted relate very closely to similar paintings by Van Gogh; that is to say, it is a direct study and the emphasis both in the way in which it has been painted and in the forms that have been given most importance is an emotional expression of the character of the tree. One recognises and recollects the particular tree in all its urgent growth and richness. In the second painting (figure 2) a similar tree has been abstracted further, not for its emotional effect but to find the sense of the structure of the tree, the interlacing of the forms, the direction of the flow and, importantly, the pattern which may be deduced from it on the surface of the canvas. Here there is still, however, something of the emotional residue of the earlier painting, but this has gone from the third picture (figure 3) which is of the same tree as the second. Here all the tendencies of the earlier abstraction have been taken to a logical limit so that little remains of the incidental painting verve and the casual treatment. What is left is a pattern of lines and interlocking tilted planes which express only the structure of the tree as understood by Mondrian. The painting is an abstraction from the tree and derives all its form from the tree. This is one form of abstraction. Here one may say that the painter has abstracted, but in so far as the derivation from the subject is clear and relative the painting will not be an abstract.

In the other use of the term, an abstract painting is one in which the shapes are not derived from a particular subject, but are put together directly from the artist's stock of experiences and his understanding of the effects of the relationships of shapes and colours. This will have no reference to the appearance of the visible world.

Examples of the two forms are found, the first in *The Three Musicians* of Picasso (plate 13) and the second in *Composition* by Mondrian (plate 42). In the former Picasso has used the figures of three musicians and their costume as a basis for the shapes he has used, as well as to derive from them the character of the painting, an eerie, wistful,

remote, sombre music only relieved by the strident note of the harlequin's costume. Another example of this kind of abstraction is found in Villon's *Little Girl at the Piano* (plate 19), the gentle interlacing of the flowing lines deriving from the young girl and the idea of the soft sweetness of the subject. Mondrian on the other hand has not started from any subject of this kind. He has tried to make a purely abstract pattern deliberately without any reference to anything in the visible world. His reasons are simple: he wishes to arrive at a pattern which expresses relationships that are found in the colours and lines themselves and that are representative of the sense of order, harmony and balance in nature. He is painting not nature but an abstraction of it (see *The nature of De Stijl and Neo-Plasticism*, page 33).

These two kinds of abstraction are easily distinguished and represent the main preoccupations of painters in this century. The ways in which they manifest themselves vary considerably; for instance an abstraction of the second kind many be seen in Kandinsky's *Black Lines* (plate 26).

Abstraction is, however, only the method, not the inspiration. The painters use it only in so far as it helps them realise their intention — to communicate their experience — and not as an end in itself. The extent of the abstraction reflects the painter's attitude to the world, to his society, to the future, to the changing character of man. The modern painter has found varying degrees of abstraction necessary to express his sense of the loss of urgency in academic art and of its lack of relevance to the way we live now, to the modern machine, to modern war, to great events, and perhaps most important, to the feeling that man himself is becoming increasingly depersonalised, subjected to the power of science which he has invented. His art is the result of an attempt, sometimes desperate, usually groping, to find a truth, an order and a faith that will allow him to live in dignity. This necessitates and inspires his new language.

From what has been said it might be imagined that abstraction is a new thing, an invention of the twentieth century. Of course this is not so; all art is in some degree abstraction. We have no space to examine this in detail, but two points must be made. Firstly, anyone who has any acquaintance with the art of the past will realise that the same subject painted by different artists produces different pictures. This is not due to different vision but to different interpretation, different response which leads to a different choice of objects of emphasis, varying artistic intentions, the one calm perhaps, and the other excited. This in turn leads to the artist laying more emphasis on some aspects of his subject, even though it is apparently painted straightforwardly, than on others. This might be classified as a temperamental abstraction. The second is a visual abstraction. A number of books have recently been written about the way in which vision is selective. When we look we do not see all that is presented to the eye; we select, or abstract, only what we need for our purpose and according to our interests. We tend to use our vision to provide us with necessary information and no more; for instance, we rarely see the grain of the wood of the door we open. We make sense of what is presented to our eyes, but that is not necessarily always what is actually there. A famous and favourite example of this is seen in the so-called Fraser spiral which is composed of concentric circles although it appears as a spiral through the deliberately created background of spiral tendency. When we make sense of something in this way, we are visually abstracting. When this is allied to temperamental abstraction one realises that there is always an unconscious abstraction at work in art.

This abstraction is different, of course, from the abstraction of modern art but it is associated with a feature which we also encounter in both modern and earlier art — distortion. The distortion of Grünewald has an obvious emotional

intention (for instance, to increase our understanding of the sense of Christ's suffering on the Cross) and this sort of distortion is frequent. Forms are created that are not directly representational but altered to achieve a pictorial effect In so far as the forms are not as seen they are abstracted, and it must be immediately apparent that this may be done for different pictorial ends; Turner's dissolved forms, Blake's heavy articulation and Constable's dots of flashing white all represent interpretative abstraction.

Nevertheless it is clear that modern abstraction is both more deliberate and more varied. It is also more exploratory, for if we examine the movements of the early years of the century we find that the intention generally has not been to present the visible world in any way that it may be seen but to use aspects of it interpretatively. In the sections dealing with the movements we shall attempt to outline the intentions of each, but it is worth while here to recollect the general circumstances in which they, for the most part, formed themselves, and to trace their ancestry.

The beginnings are to be discerned in the academic traditions of the nineteenth century which held without question or challenge the aesthetic standards developed during the Renaissance. Before the end of the century, first the Impressionists and later the Post-Impressionists had so effectively attacked this aesthetic that it was clear that eventually it would be superseded. The principles of Renaissance art had become so debased through the centuries of repetition that in the nineteenth century in France, where the beginnings of the artistic revolution are to be found, a painting could be described as a construction of figures posed in heroic attitudes illustrating particular events from history or mythology. Painting had become an intellectual exercise removed from experience of nature.

The inadequacy of this debilitated aesthetic became apparent to some young students in the middle years of the century, and it was through them that a new interest in the physical aspect of the world began to appear in painting. The Impressionists discarded most of what the academics held dear, 'heroic' subject-matter, tonal composition (i. e. the building of the picture in light and dark), static constructed composition, and interested themselves in the everyday life of the people of France and the landscape surrounding them. Instead of the heavy dark painting — the result of tonal construction — they used a lighter colour range in their examination and observation of life and the effect of light on the moving landscape. Their art was largely observational and cared more for the temporary appearance of things in a particular light than for the emotive possibilities of their subject. This was the concern of the Post-Impressionists who were interested in the emotional possibilities of the commonplace or the sense of order that landscape or figure presented. Van Gogh, when he painted the *Yellow Chair*, was not only concerned with its appearance but with the possibility it presented as a mould for intense feeling about the physical world. Cézanne, when he painted *Mont Ste Victoire*, was concerned with the ordered world it represented to him.

The diminished concern with subject led to a diminished interest in the actual appearance of the visible world and an increased interest in what it represented to the artist's temperament. From this emerged a concern with the picture that was being painted rather than with the subject it might be depicting; subject became subordinated to the painting itself. Thus the arrangement of colours which had always before been 'a horse, a nude or some sort of anecdote' began to stand for the artist's understanding of or emotional response to nature without necessarily using any single place or actual person. The tendency towards picture surface abstraction, which has continued through the twentieth century, had begun. Most of the modern art movements,

including all that we are considering, contain examples.

Into this atmosphere at the end of the nineteenth century were born the young painters who were to create the modern movements. There was still the academic tradition of 'historical' and portrait painting, which maintained its hold on the established culture and society, and there was also the new non-academic art still seeming, as the opening quotation shows, outrageous and ridiculous.

To many people there seemed to be no reason why the Victorian age, representing in its name the dominance of England and her industries throughout the nineteenth century, should not continue for ever, believing in itself and its righteousness. In the first two decades of the following century, however, this supremacy was shattered. Europe was plunged into a decimating war, the industrial example of England was being copied and extended throughout Europe, America showed her potential dominance in world affairs, the Russian revolution revealed the power of the Communist idea, radio, the motor car and the aeroplane revolutionised communications. The first World War tore the countries of Europe apart, killed or maimed millions of all sorts and abilities, and fractured the society of the pre-war years which had no conception of its terrifying power, limitless destruction and universal grief; through countless personal tragedies it produced a Europe which could never forget the possibility of war's recurrence. At the same time the years before the war seemed full of potential — a new century, the twentieth, could look forward to an industrial expansion, an age of plenty, an age of the new machine.

The young artists at the turn of the century were sensitive to this new atmosphere and nowhere more than in Paris which, as a result of the acceptance by the critics (but not yet by all the public) of the art of the Impressionists and their successors, had become the art capital of the world. To it all young aspiring artists gravitated, from Germany,

Italy, Spain, England and even America. Enthusiasm, energy and talent accumulated, and in the cafés the infusion of other nationals took the discussion of art theories beyond the old boundaries and opened up new possibilities. European art began to take on an international flavour opposed to the old national academies. It was a time of great excitement for the young painter and it engaged all his energies. At the same time in other parts of Europe the example of Paris was followed, and revolutionary groups were formed which were antipathetic to the traditional art and reacting to the atmosphere of possibility in the new century.

They searched for a pictorial language that could express their feelings about the developing society. The academies depressed them; the instruction was too firmly rooted in the previous century to excite them or inspire them and they turned naturally to the anti-academic painters of the older generation. Of these they found the greatest inspiration in Paul Cézanne with whom all consideration of modern art must begin. Basil Taylor opens a recent essay on Cézanne by saying that he 'has been the patron-hero of painting for at least the first forty years of our century, and while his works have the same kind of status in the history of art as Masaccio's frescoes in the Brancacci Chapel or the Sistine ceiling, it is perhaps the power of his presence and the virility of his ideals, more than the example of any single picture, which has inspired artists whose intention and practice have been quite different from his own.' One may imagine how powerful was his influence in the first years of the century when he was still alive. A great regard for his independence and the distinction of his work was part of the *avant-garde* feeling in Paris. He was given a whole room in the Autumn Salon of 1904, was represented again in 1905 and 1906, and in 1907 a memorial exhibition was arranged. The basis of this regard lay in the inspiration he gave to the young painters in their search for a new language of art, particularly in respect of his emphasis on the canvas surface as part of the picture. Although he dealt with the visible aspects of nature he was concerned to find in each 'motif' the underlying sense of order in nature which he felt could be expressed independently of the limitless space before his eyes or of the convention of perspective. This led him to try slowly, laboriously and sensitively to build the relationships he found into paint relationships, building up a limited and controlled space on the flat surface of the canvas which, for him, could contain the order he found. He was so successful that his influence is found in all aspects of the modern developments in painting.

Paris was the centre for the earliest movements. Fauvism, led by Matisse, was the first to appear and caused some outcry in the press in 1905 and 1906. As the public had not at that time fully accepted the work of Van Gogh, were only just becoming aware of Gauguin and dismissed Cézanne as an incompetent, it is not surprising that they failed to understand what the Fauves were attempting. Hardly had the noise from Fauvism subsided when an even more outrageous movement appeared, led by Picasso — Cubism. The public at large has never really recovered from its assault, and one might say that it was at this point that suspicion, doubt and despondency set in which have never really been dissipated. (It accounts, too, for the unique position held by Picasso. His restless, flamboyant spirit and his obvious fitness as leader of the *avant-garde* has led to a prevailing suspicion that he is responsible for the whole of modern art.) The appearance of Cubism extended the influence of Paris. Fauvism had had some influence on Expressionism, the modern German movement then growing, but the effect of Cubism was much more widespread. German Expressionism incorporated it in the second wave of its development, the Blue Rider group; Italian Futurism depended upon it for at least part of its pictorial language; in England a group known as the Vorticists, led by Wyndham Lewis and William Roberts, derived in part from it; Mondrian made it the basis of his art in 1911 and for some years afterwards, and innumerable independents followed or extended it. It was the beginning of the new art and divided the public into two groups as never before; there was incomprehension and intolerance on both sides, the *avant-garde* unable to believe that the academics could carry on as before with the vista of liberty and artistic adventure opening before them, while the academics could not conceive that the *avant-garde* was serious, knew what it was doing, or had a proper respect for art. The rift included the artists themselves who violently took sides. This led to a modern phenomenon, the art manifesto, and to professional critics who interpreted the obscure or threw up a hedge of words around the work of the moderns.

Most of the later movements issued manifestoes and explanatory documents rightly supposing that they would not be accepted on their work alone and incidentally revealing an intellectual preoccupation. In the first three decades of the century Apollinaire published a defence of Cubism (1913), Matisse published *Notes of a Painter* (1908), G. Duthuit wrote *Fauvism* (1929—31), Marinetti published the first Futurist manifesto (1909), Van Doesburg issued the magazine *De Stijl* (1917), Kandinsky produced *The Blue Rider* (1911) and published *Concerning the Spiritual in Art* in 1912, the English Vorticists published their manifesto in a magazine *Blast* (1914), and André Breton issued the first Surrealist manifesto (1924). The flood of writings grew and the academic critics replied with their own attacks and defences. It was a period of excitement which probably only those who participated in it could appreciate.

These activities were accompanied by great energy on the part of the painters which resulted in the production of so much work that even an eager and sympathetic market could not easily have absorbed it. Such a market at that time the moderns could not find and they were obliged to create their own means of showing their work — the dealers were not unnaturally a little diffident about accepting everything that was produced. They set up seasonal exhibitions, like the Autumn Salon which first appeared in 1903, to show their work and they sold at very low prices. Even so, large numbers lived in extreme want and furthered the notion that this is the way that artists like to live — *la vie de bohème*, in fact. This had the effect of producing two art societies, the official and dignified, and the *avant-garde* and squalid. Since then this notion has led to the expectation that the artist wishes to live outside society and is irresponsible and unkempt. This in turn has attracted the irresponsible and unwashed would-be artist and preserves the division, unwanted by the true artist, between him and the rest of society.

Another result of this divorce of the modern artist and society is the unfortunate belief that it is the sole aim of the artist to ridicule or attack society and that it is consequently the duty of society to defend itself. The gulf between the artist and the society in which he lives results in an uneasy relationship, sometimes of tolerance, sometimes of amusement, sometimes of envy but usually of suspicion and mistrust on both sides. Anything which contributes towards a greater measure of understanding on either side should help to narrow the gulf and eventually produce a greater understanding, appreciation and enjoyment of works of art.

If this short introduction can do anything towards showing the essential seriousness of the artist and the possibility of his contributing something of value to the community he lives in, it will have served its turn. Unless society learns to value its artists, that vulgarisation and mediocrity, lack of sensitivity and exaltation of the mundane which is becoming increasingly evident will eventually swamp it.

FAUVISM

The artists

Henri Matisse 1869—1954

Albert Marquet 1875—1947

Henri-Charles Manguin 1874—1949

Charles Camoin 1879—

Jean Puy 1876—1960

André Derain 1880—1954

Maurice Vlaminck 1876—1958

Othon Friesz 1879—1949

Louis Valtat 1869—1952

Raoul Dufy 1877—1953

Georges Braque 1882—1963

The Fauves, like most twentieth-century art associations, were casually held together by a general similarity of outlook. The painters were not bound by theory as much as by temperament and soon dispersed to develop individually. The undoubted leader was Matisse although Vlaminck, an extrovert personality given to extravagant gestures, has claimed the invention of Fauvism.

Pictorial characteristics

The pictorial characteristics of Fauvism are an excited and highly exaggerated use of colour, with perspective and subject matter of the Impressionists (landscapes, still life, figures in commonplace action).

The name

Essentially a French and primarily a Parisian art movement, the name 'Fauves' to describe the painters has a certain relevance. It is French for 'wild beasts' and was coined by the art critic Louis Vauxcelles as a disparaging comment on the extravagant, vivid and turbulent paintings that the group exhibited in the Autumn Salon of 1906. They had been given a room to themselves, and the hanging committee, doubtless with the hope of softening the effect of this violent work on the walls, had placed a number of small academic sculptures in the middle of the room. One of these by the sculptor Marque of a small standing figure provoked Vauxcelles to remark *Donatello parmi les fauves* ('Donatello amongst the wild beasts', or perhaps, by implication, 'Daniel in the lions' den').

The name caught on and thereafter the painters were known as Fauves. Whilst of course it is an irrelevant name, in fact it does contain a reference to the exuberant and irreverent character of this form of painting, its refusal to conform and its strident voice.

The origins and development

Fauvism as a movement had a short life, really only between 1905 and 1907. Its origins and the influences which moulded it can be traced back to the beginning of the century and to the career of Matisse during these years.

After a short and unhappy period studying under the academic painter Bouguereau, Matisse entered the studio of Gustave Moreau, equally academic but, strangely, a more inspiring teacher. Whilst there he met Marquet, Manguin, Camoin and Puy. When Moreau died in 1898 the group dispersed; but Matisse was already the dominating influence and, when he returned from a year in the south of France and Corsica with some strongly coloured canvases and sketches with some pointilliste characteristics, the others adopted, with some caution, his vivid new method. Pointillisme, the invention of Seurat, depends for its effectiveness on the mixing of colour not on the canvas but, as it were, in the eye. Small dots are placed closely side by side so that at a distance they will fuse into one colour (blue and yellow dots will give green). Seurat's followers did not maintain the physically exhausting method and used larger spots of colour which did not mix optically but nevertheless gave a similar colour sensation. It was one of these followers, Signac, who fired Matisse with enthusiasm for this extension of pointillisme which later became for a time a feature of Fauvism. With the Fauves, however, the small spots became larger and dabs, which often followed the direction of the form, became more vigorous, thus linking pointillisme with Van Gogh.

About this time (1900) Derain met the self-taught Vlaminck, both of whom lived at Chatou near Paris, and was excited by his work. To capture the exuberance they felt in front of the rich landscape they applied paint straight from the tube, with all its fullness of colour unadulterated by mixing.

In 1901 a great retrospective exhibition of Van Gogh's work was held in Paris, and all the young painters who were later to become Fauves found it a stunning revelation of the ideas they were then evolving. At this exhibition Matisse was introduced to Vlaminck by Derain, and the circle around Matisse thus expanded.

During the next two years Vlaminck continued to paint the strongly coloured landscapes under the impetus of Van Gogh, while Matisse and his group concentrated on quieter paintings in which line was used to divide forms. During this time three young painters, Othon Friesz, Dufy and Braque, came from Le Havre to Paris and joined the association.

There were two important group shows open to young and *avant-garde* painters by 1903: the Salon of Independent Painters (Salon des Indépendants) founded in 1884 and having no selection committee, and the Autumn Salon (Salon d'Automne) founded in 1903 with a selection committee intended only to keep out the incompetent and the crank. It was to the Autumn Salon after 1903 that the Fauves mostly sent their paintings, and in 1905 their first impact as a group was felt. The work of Matisse and Derain particularly attracted attention. They had spent the summer painting together at Collioure, a village just south of Perpignan, and their brilliant neo-pointilliste paintings were a considerable shock to the public. Most of the group exhibited, including Marquet, Manguin, Friesz, Puy, Valtat and Vlaminck. We should also note that Kandinsky and Jawlensky exhibited in this Salon (see *Expressionism*, page 22).

In 1904 several exhibitions of importance to the Fauves had taken place in Paris: a memorial exhibition to Gauguin, whose ideas about the use of colour inspired them; an exhibition of French Primitives; a first show of Mohammedan art, greatly admired by Matisse; and a large retrospective exhibition of Manet, who was regarded as the first to bridge the gap between perception and expression (discussed in the Introduction).

In 1906 Fauvism as a group movement was born. In the Autumn Salon all the Fauves exhibited and they acquired their name. They were also given some press publicity including press reproductions of what were thought to be the most outrageous works — *The Green Stripe* (plate 2) was one. At this time the German group of Expressionists were working along the same lines and there seemed every likelihood that Fauvism would become an international painting style.

At the height of its *avant-garde* success in 1907, when it was beginning to attract wider attention, another development which was to become Cubism began to supercede Fauvism.

After this the group dispersed, pursuing independent lines of development.

Another influence on the Fauves is the all-important

Cézanne. His bather paintings had captured Matisse's imagination and in 1898 he had bought one which remained for him, as he said, a 'constant source of spiritual sustenance' for forty years.

The history of Fauvism thereafter is one of individual development along separate lines. Matisse remains the most significant of them although several of the others became well known. Dufy's charming colour was extraordinarily popular; Derain and Braque became Cubists; Vlaminck became more wildly attached to the emotional possibility of paint and his later work comes closer to German Expressionism.

The nature of Fauvism

Fauvism is essentially the result of an enthusiasm and exuberance in respect of colour. As we have seen in the Introduction, the Impressionists and their immediate successors showed that, whatever the subject-matter of the painting and however 'accurate' the presentation of appearance, no painters prior to the Impressionists had used colour with the freedom and variety of effect of which it was capable. Colour could be used to turn the most prosaic and apparently ordinary subject into a source of inspiration and pleasure. With the Impressionists this exploration of colour became part of the *raison d'être* of a work and only infrequently did the significance of the painting extend beyond this. With their successors the emotional significance of the subject involved a special use of colour to express this extended meaning and, as we have noted, in Van Gogh, Cézanne and Seurat the Fauves found an inspiration for their own personal use of colour.

Fauvist subject-matter is essentially Impressionist and Post-Impressionist in character. A Fauvist painter takes a scene, a landscape or a figure and paints it without deliberate distortion of ordinary perspective. The interest in the subject is always nostalgic and is always easily identifiable. Derain's

Pool of London (plate 4), painted probably in the autumn of 1906, is a good example of this. It is only in the colour that liberties have been taken; for the rest, it is a conventional perspective view. The other painting by Derain illustrated in this book, a brilliant portrait of Matisse (plate 5), makes the same point in respect of a head. Although the colour is elaborated the drawing is basically academic. What separates this and all Fauvism from academic painting is that on this academic framework the colour 'orchestration' expresses space through the inherent qualities of different colours, depending on colour 'notes' rather than on tone.

The violence and intensity of colour in Fauvism is nowhere more strongly expressed than in the painting of Vlaminck, of which *Les Bâteaux-Lavoirs* (plate 8) is a representative example. The colour here is not what would have been seen in ordinary vision. Vlaminck explains: 'I used to go to work right out in the sunshine; the sky was blue, the wheatfields seemed to be stirring and trembling in the torrid heat, with hues of yellow covering the whole scale of chromes; they quivered as if they were about to pop up in flames. Vermilion alone could render the brilliant red of the roof tiles on the hillside across the river. The orange of the soil, the raw harsh colours of walls and grass, the ultramarine and cobalt of the sky, harmonised to extravagance at a sensual musical pitch. Only the colours on my canvas, orchestrated to the limit of their power and resonance, could render the colour emotions of that landscape.' Emotion and naturalism — that is the character of Vlaminck's art as revealed in this passage.

As well as from enthusiasm for colour, Fauvism stems also from a belief that colour relationships have an effect as pure colour quite apart from their effect as a colour attached to a particular object — we have already noticed this in the Introduction. Gauguin heightened the colour of the areas of his painting in relation to each other in an attempt to give each colour value its maximum significance. In *The Green Stripe* (plate 2), at first sight visually ridiculous, the stripe becomes both an expressive element and a unifying agent when the colour relationships impinge upon the sensibility. There is a warm and a cold side to the face which the intense green, neither warm nor cold, unifies. The green also serves to increase the luminosity of its near complementary reds, to emphasise the cold green, and, through its colour quality, advance towards the spectator and give volume to the head.

In the more Expressionist, emotional self-portrait (plate 1) green is again used to give volume and in this picture one sees something of the influence of Cézanne in the handling of planes for the careful building of form. The treatment is nevertheless extremely forceful and the linear pattern predominates. This painting may be described as a proto-Fauvist work.

A further point, true of both these portraits, may be made. At a deeper level the unusual power of Matisse is shown in the tension between the colours themselves which evokes an atmosphere, an emotional response, independently of the form of the subject and revealing the character of each subject.

The influence of Fauvism on subsequent painting is also important since it presages the autonomous use of colour in the abstract work later in this century. Colour, we have suggested, can have an emotional effect independent of any relation with subject-matter. In later years Matisse, and to some extent Dufy, moved towards this kind of use of colour, operating only on the surface, achieving its effect with little outside reference, becoming, effectively, an emotional experience in colour relationship. The Divisionist technique of Matisse's *Luxe, Calme et Volupté* (plate 3) deriving from his association with Signac, does not disguise the essential perspective naturalism of his treatment. In Dufy's painting *Promenade au Quai* (plate 7) the form derives from the colour 'orchestration' of natural objects with the interest centred on the intensity with which colour may be expressed.

A characteristic of Fauvism revealed in the scene of *Le Pont-Neuf* (plate 6) by Marquet is its constant search for the colourful image. The casual drawing, excited brush strokes and sharp areas of colour are typical of Fauvism.

One notes that Marquet has treated the scene in acceptable perspective and in this common characteristic of Fauvism we find the reason for the wide acceptance of the movement.

CUBISM

The artists

Pablo Picasso 1881—
Georges Braque 1882—1963
Juan Gris 1887—1927
Fernand Léger 1881—1955
Louis Marcoussis 1883—1941
Albert Gleizes 1881—1953
Jean Metzinger 1883—1957
Robert Delaunay 1885—1941
Jacques Villon 1875—1963
Marcel Duchamp 1887—

Although all the painters listed above had some association with Cubism and at some time during the early years of the century could be included in a list of Cubists, the most important in the formation of the ideas and techniques associated with the movement are Picasso and Braque. Gris and Léger hold the next most important formative positions in that they explored paths indicated by Picasso and Braque. Delaunay, Duchamp and Villon are Cubists only in some characteristics.

All the most important Cubists, including Picasso and Braque, moved from Cubism proper to other forms of painting, most of them before the First World War.

Pictorial characteristics

Great variation occurs in the appearance of Cubist paintings, but they are all in some degree distortions of the visible world and not invented abstracts. They do not use the conventional perspective, or realist colour, nor do they necessarily conform to a single viewpoint. The resultant paintings may vary from small interlocking facets or planes in dull (grey-green or brown) colour to bold patterns of large shapes in strong non-realist colour.

The name

Cubism was primarily a Parisian art movement deriving from the inquisitive energy of the atmosphere of Paris at the turn of the century. Like Fauvism, the name was coined by the art critic Louis Vauxcelles, when he referred to the paintings of Braque in 1908 as composed of *cubes* and in the following year as *bizarreries cubiques*. Matisse is also said to have described Braque's paintings as made of *petits cubes*. Thereafter the term became widely known and was used to describe paintings only remotely connected with Cubism — indeed any paintings that seemed *avant-garde*. In 1913 the critic and writer Guillaume Apollinaire attempted the first assessment of the group under the title *The Cubist Painters* and by this time the term was generally current. It is, of course, somewhat misleading and lays emphasis on only one aspect of Cubism which was not in any case the basic idea. It is as well not to try to deduce anything of the character of Cubism from its name.

The origins and character

The movement lasted from about 1908 to the beginnings of the First World War in 1914. After this war the painters returned to Paris and renewed acquaintances (most of them had served in the army). They began painting again in the Cubist manner, but the original urgency had dissolved and a coherent movement could not be reformed. Some painters like Metzinger, Gris and Gleizes, remained Cubist, some new adherents were acquired, some painters toyed with Cubism for short periods, and some adapted some of its ideas to their own purposes. As a result it is reasonable to claim that Cubism has been the most influential of the twentieth-century art movements.

It was also the earliest of the obviously iconoclastic revolutionary movements in that, unlike its predecessor Fauvism, it attacked practically all the accepted standards and notions of painting.

One of the great masterpieces of twentieth-century painting, the large canvas known as *Les Demoiselles d'Avignon* (plate 9) by Picasso can be said to have inaugurated Cubism with an explosive assertion. In this painting, started in 1906 and unfinished in 1907 when it was seen by Braque, Picasso introduced a number of ideas about the whole possibility of painting. We shall later see the nature of these innovations but we should note here the impact that they had upon a number of younger painters in Paris and particularly on Braque. They also established Picqsso as the leader of the *avant-garde* superseding Matisse and Fauvism.

From late in 1909 for the next few years Picasso joined with Braque in an association so close that the work of either painter is only distinguishable by the experienced student, and together they worked out the form of Cubism. In 1911 they were joined by Gris, like Picasso a Spaniard who had gravitated to Paris, and between 1908 and 1911 Cubist methods were adopted by numerous young painters not all of whom understood what it was all about and whose work, although of historical interest, is not of any great importance.

The first concerted public display of Cubist painting occurred in the Salon des Indépendants of 1911. In Room 41 (this has become the well-known descriptive term for the show) most of the leading Cubists except Picasso and Braque, who were rarely to be seen in exhibitions at this time, formed a group who were attacked by the press. Those exhibiting included Léger, Gleizes, Delaunay and Metzinger, and only Apollinaire defended them. The adverse criticism, however, had, as so often, the effect of increasing public interest, and the show was always crowded. Cubism became the *avant-garde* fashion.

In 1912 Cubism spread beyond the boundaries of France: Cubists were represented in the Blue Rider exhibition in Munich (see *Expressionism*, page 22), in Cologne, in Berlin, Zürich, Moscow, Barcelona and at the Grafton Galleries in London.

In the following year new tendencies and directions in Cubism began to appear — particularly important is Orphism, the creation of Delaunay. Since we shall have no opportunity of discussing this later we may say here that Orphism derived from analytical Cubism (discussed below, page 21), its followers believing that the Cubists' use of colour was too limited and depended too much on the subject. This led to Delaunay's propounding his own theories of colour under the heading of 'Simultaneous Contrasts' and to painting that was almost entirely abstract.

At this time too the influence of Cubism is found in other movements beginning throughout Europe. The Italian Futurist movement, the Dutch group known as De Stijl, the Russian Constructivists, the English Vorticists and the German Expressionist group, the Blue Riders, all owed something to the Cubist revolution.

During the 1920s and into the 1930s the influence of Cubism persisted and Picasso, who had by this time in his meteoric progress changed the character of his art several times, reverted to it occasionally or extended its possibilities in directions not until then explored. Braque, a slower and less volatile personality, continued to use Cubism and to investigate its possibilities in subtle variations.

At the present moment the influence of Cubism is still discernible in the work of large numbers of painters who are possibly themselves unaware of it, indeed, this influence is extended beyond the boundaries of art itself.

The nature of Cubism

It must first be reiterated that Cubism is not a descriptive term: Cubist painters do not paint in cubes. Nor is the quotation from Cézanne so often adduced as the basis of Cubist inspiration as significant in Cubist thought as is supposed. Cézanne in a letter to Emile Bernard in 1904 wrote: 'May I repeat what I told you here: treat nature by the cylinder, the sphere, the cone, everything in proper perspective so that each side of an object or a plane is directed towards a central point.' This has been used to support the idea that the Cubists simplified forms to the nearest approach to these forms that was possible. Examination of any Cubist painting will not bear this out.

It would be more illuminating if we were to remember that this was a movement of young men in their twenties in the heady atmosphere of Paris. As we have suggested in the Introduction these young men felt profound dissatisfaction with the whole character of the nineteenth-century legacy of painting. They wanted something different, something that seemed to express the new age, not an art whose greatest ambition was to get into the museums and sit beside the past in unexceptionable comity. This meant experiment, attack and exploration, preceded by a new visual excitement about the possibilities of unregarded art, of Negro art, of Cézanne, of the primitive painter, Douanier Rousseau, as well as about the new theories of colour which had not long been formulated.

In this light, Cubism appears as a young, excited experiment without, at least in the first instance, any very clearly formulated notions. When we remember the subsequent career of Picasso and his restless inquisitive spirit, this becomes an obviously probable genesis. Further, if we examine the examples illustrated, which range from 1907 to 1921, we cannot discern any overriding intellectual idea determining the forms. What seems more apparent is variety and casualness; there is no desire to create what might be described as a Work of Art fit for the museums, but a determination to find out what can be done within a very loose framework of ideas if the normal limitations of art are not observed. By these limitations we mean the whole standard of Renaissance and post-Renaissance art down to the nineteenth century. Discarding these standards opened up new possibilities for these young painters. They no longer had to be concerned with classical beauty and proportion. Were there not valuable qualities of proportion apart from the classical ones, did not Negro art obviously obey different laws and was it not of a more urgent directness? Did they have to observe their subject-matter, as had the art of the past, from one point of view and at one moment in time? Could they not incorporate different possible points of view in one picture? Had they even to obey the whole previous idea about space? Had they always to regard the flatness of the surface of the canvas as something which must be destroyed in the process of creating the illusion of space — of a box behind the frame? They had, as we have seen in the Introduction, a precedent for at least rethinking this question, for Cézanne had already recreated the concern for surface and suggested a new possibility of space presentation.

The course of Cubism, if viewed basically as exploratory and building upon pictorial discovery during this exploration, becomes more intelligible and much more exciting. It also creates a new atmosphere for picture making. The visible world, as it always does, remains the inspiration for these painters but the picture ceases to be a mnemonic for nature and exists as something that is searched or appreciated for its own qualities independent of nature.

What are the qualities and discoveries of the Cubists? Examination of the plates will reveal at least a few of them as well as showing the course of the movement in its various forms.

Les Demoiselles d'Avignon (plate 9) is, as already indicated, one of the important documents of the movement. It is still uncompleted and is thus unresolved as a composition. It shows the influences of Iberian sculpture in the three left-hand figures, of Negro sculpture in the two right-hand figures, and of Cézanne throughout the whole work. There is an attempt to divide the surface into a series of vertical forms and, deriving from Cézanne, to create a solidity in the figures without a simple consistent space. Here the picture has become a surface of action, an integration of shapes, an amalgamation of pictorial ideas not entirely interrelated or worked out. This painting is a prototype for Cubism rather than a complete expression of it.

It began the analysis of form into simpler elements and the relation of those elements in a pictorial plan on the canvas surface using only a limited space. This became a feature of the next stage in the development of Cubism which is usually described as 'analytical Cubism', a name given by Gris as an indication of the increasing breakdown of form. Picasso's *Seated Woman* (plate 10), and *Ma Jolie* (plate 11), and Braque's *The Portuguese* (plate 14) are all important examples. In *Seated Woman* the main shapes of the body may still be discerned but they have been broken down into a number of facets which interlock with each other and present a sort of moving articulation like the surface of crumpled or folded paper, as when we make a paper hat from a flat sheet. It is an examination of the way in which the forms themselves articulate but, still more, it is a testing of the pictorially possible. In this picture (and this is also true of the Braque) Picasso has discovered a way of uniting a three-dimensional effect in the subject with the flatness of the surface and at the same time suggesting something of the careful restraint of a Cézanne landscape. In *Ma Jolie* the process is extended so that the subject — in this case a figure with a guitar — is almost lost in the small facets that are created

in the extensive breakdown of form. The result is a more conscious disintegration of the subject and a consequent increase in the awareness of surface forms.

Braque, the son of a house-painting contractor, was familiar with the materials of this trade, and the next stage in Cubist development arose from an interest in the variety of surface reproductions (wood, graining, beading, pebble) available in wallpapers, etc. — as well as actual materials. Picasso and Braque in 1911 had become interested in the rendering of surface textures in the still-life groups that they were engaged in and they began to apply these textures rather than paint them. They also attached pieces of newspapers to their canvases, and even made relief sculptures of wood and plaster. These arose from a developing interest in colour and form on the surface rather than the analysis of volume. The result became a new kind of decorative painting — analytical and balanced and with a new colour sophistication. There was, at this stage, less excitement and more reflection. This is well shown in Picasso's *The Violin* (plate 12) and Braque's *Bottle, Glass and Pipe* (plate 15). The decorative possibilities of this more sophisticated Cubism are seen in *The Three Musicians* (plate 13). We have also mentioned in respect of this painting its haunting power, for there is not only a decorative element, but also a sombre music in the forms and their relationship.

The character of Cubism also owes a great deal to Gris, whose quieter nature was more balanced and orderly than Picasso's and simpler and more direct than Braque's. Of his paintings the *Still Life in Front of an Open Window* (plate 16) is a good example; the analysis is more consistent, more controlled, less urgent, and the results are paintings of colour balance and harmony of a visually satisfying kind. Gris established the pictorial validity of many aspects of Cubism.

Marcel Duchamp's *Nude Descending a Staircase* (plate 18) is not solely a Cubist painting and shows how stimulating and inspiring Cubism proved to be. Here Duchamp is using the analytical aspect of Cubism as a means of expressing sequential movement. Several stages in a figure's descent of a few stairs are interlocked in one painting; it is no longer concerned with one point in time. This preoccupation with the time element is a feature of the Italian movement, Futurism, which is considered later, and this painting had considerable influence upon the Futurists as well as being one of the most effective expressions of the idea. Marcel Duchamp himself is a most influential figure in the history of modern painting, for his work, as well as having Cubist and Futurist characteristics, was also an important part of Surrealism.

The Wedding (plate 17) by Léger is not typical of the familiar work of this painter who later developed a geometric form of painting which, deriving partly from Cubism, expressed his extraordinarily rich sense of pattern and a kind of humanist sympathy with the machine age. This painting shows Léger's concern with volumes expressed more solidly than in Picasso or Braque, as well as his different treatment of the open and closed space. His work is also of a more literary and allegorical order.

In the work of all these Cubists we see disrespect for the established order and an inquisitiveness which has opened up for modern painting new possibilities of visual experience. It is the Cubists whom we must commend for this enlargement — or, of course, condemn, if our sensibilities direct us to it, for the ruination of art.

EXPRESSIONISM

The artists

Edvard Munch 1863—1944
Christian Rohlfs 1849—1938
Ernst Ludwig Kirchner 1880—1938
Erich Heckel 1883—
Carl Schmidt-Rottluff 1884—
Otto Mueller 1874—1930
Emil Nolde 1867—1956
Max Pechstein 1881—1955
Wassily Kandinsky 1866—1944
Franz Marc 1880—1916
Paul Klee 1879—1940
August Macke 1887—1914
Heinrich Campendonk 1889—1957
Alexei von Jawlensky 1864—1941
Max Beckmann 1844—1950
Lyonel Feininger 1871—1956
Oscar Kokoschka 1886—

This list, longer than those for the other movements, is still by no means exhaustive although it includes most of the more important Expressionist painters. This is predominately a German group and the list does not include the German precursors like Max Slevogt or Lovis Corinth. It is mainly concerned with those painters who participated in the two movements in Germany which parallel French Fauvism, Die Brücke (The Bridge) in Dresden and Der Blaue Reiter (The Blue Rider) in Munich, although some independent Expressionists are included.

Pictorial characteristics

The characteristics of Expressionist painting are similar to those of Fauvism, except that Expressionist painters tend to use stronger linear effects, more heavy colour (black and browns), with the object of expressing the sense of tension in life that they felt.

The name

Expressionism as a term has a number of associations and may be used in a wider sense than we are using it here. In its broadest sense it may be used to describe widely differing works from various periods in history as well as the present which exhibit only a strong emotional content in common. In the historical sense this is the use to which the term is put. In another and more limited sense the term may be used to describe all art since Impressionism which has found the Impressionists' lack of involvement a limitation and which, as a result, laid stress on intuition and emotion. In this sense it includes the work of Gauguin, Van Gogh and the Fauves (see page 14).

The sense in which it is used here is, however, limited to the German manifestation of the form of art.

Origins and development

Expressionism, in common with Fauvism, has its roots in the Post-Impressionist antagonism to the Impressionists' lack of emotional commitment. It derives at least part of its inspiration from the work of the Fauves with whom it had come into contact through Kandinsky and Jawlensky in Paris in 1905.

Whilst the birth of Cubism in France signalled the death of the short-lived movement of Fauvism, Expressionism in Germany flourished and absorbed some aspects of Cubism in its course. The vitality of Expressionism in Germany may, at least in part, be attributed to the strongly emotional national temperament which has resulted in the predominance of harshness, power and tension over charm and seductive appeal. Expressionism is the art of emotion, revealing inner human tensions.

In nineteenth-century German art there were a number of painters whose work, academic in character, nevertheless exhibits Expressionist characteristics and it is from these that the first important twentieth-century movement springs. Most of the early Expressionists were pupils or followers of these men.

Edvard Munch, a Norwegian who spent some time in Germany during a morose wander round Europe, was an important influence. This morbid, neurotic painter is an early symbol of the uneasy, tragic, taut but forceful nature of the whole movement. Munch's early life was unhappy and dogged by misfortune; he developed a fear of life and a mistrust of love and expressed this in a number of heavy, resigned, pessimistic works.

During his years in Germany Munch met and influenced most of the painters who were to form Die Brücke. This group, which was the first to form, came together in Dresden in 1905 under the leadership of Kirchner to make a more cohesive unit than their French counterparts, the Fauves. Less well known than the later Blue Riders, at least outside Germany, they were none the less extremely important in its prewar culture and remained a closely organised group, exhibiting and studying together until their dissolution just prior to the beginning of the war. The members were Kirchner, Heckel, Nolde, Pechstein, Schmidt-Rottluff and Otto Mueller; of these Kirchner, Mueller and Nolde remained Expressionist after the war. The name and the purpose of the group were explained by Schmidt-Rottluff as forming a bridge to convey across it all the revolutionary elements which were in gestation and to provide the direction for the future.

In 1911 the Blue Rider group began and held its first exhibition at the end of the year. The name arose from the association of Kandinsky and Marc: 'We both loved blue; Marc loved horses, and I riders; and thus the name arose by itself.' The important members apart from Kandinsky and Marc were Jawlensky, Macke, Campendonk, Klee and the composer Arnold Schönberg. They were never as closely organised a group as The Bridge, though the publication of a Blue Rider almanac by Kandinsky and Marc helped to create an identity for the group, and Kandinsky published in 1912 the most important of its documents and one of the most interesting of modern writings on the nature of art. The movement was, however, short-lived since the First World War intervened, Marc and Macke were killed, Kandinsky went back to his native Russia and Klee was in the army. After the war Klee and Kandinsky joined the Bauhaus and thereafter their careers are bound up with teaching.

Apart from these two groups there are a number of independent or loosely associated artists who should be mentioned. Lyonel Feininger, who exhibited with the Blue Rider, was not a member and his work is more closely allied to Cubism than it is to the German Expressionist character. Max Beckmann's, on the other hand, typifies a certain protesting aspect of Expressionism. His war experiences induced in him a concern for the terrible power that man possesses without a corresponding sense of responsibility in wielding it; his art, as a result, is a harsh heavy symbolism of shapes in strong black lines. It is searching and direct — both qualities to be seen in the *Self Portrait* (plate 33). Oskar Kokoschka, born in Austria, is essentially an independent character who has spent a large part of his life outside his native country and now lives in Switzerland. His art, perhaps the most vivid and sensitive of all the German Expressionists, is well represented by his early masterpiece *The Tempest* (plate 30; sometimes known as *The Vortex*).

The character of Expressionism

Something has already been said of Fauvism about the emotional basis of much early twentieth-century painting. German Expressionism is different from its French counterpart in several significant ways. The German temperament has always turned towards the mystical and emotional; it has always seemed to have a serious creative urge, an enquiring spirituality, a sense of human destiny, quite different from the delicacy, charm and sense of humour which we associate with France. The main differences between Fauvism and German Expressionism arise from this contrast in character. Whereas Fauvism developed into a more decorative and charming display of colour, the German movement became increasingly mystical and socially conscious; it philosophised and delved deeper into possibilities of abstract expression avoided by the French. In fact, the later movement, the Blue Rider, owes at least as much of its form to Cubism. The paintings of Marc, Macke and even to some extent Jawlensky show its effect. With Marc this is a predominant aspect if we compare *The Fate of Animals* (plate 27) with the Gris *Still Life* (plate 16) or with Villon's *Little Girl at the Piano* (plate 19). The main distinctions lie in the character of the subject. In both the Cubist examples there is observational analysis without great emotional implication, whereas the Marc springs from a strong feeling for the terror that lurks in the forest. The Marc is strident and harsh, while the Gris and the Villon are quiet, reflective and charming.

The Bridge group, with only the vague call to action which Kirchner later embodied in a woodcut, had no deliberate policy and the work of its members differed considerably in intention and quality. The influence of Munch was omnipresent and the nature of that influence can be seen in *The Dance of Life* (plate 20) which is impregnated with symbolism, built up of pessimistic heavy forms, introspective and tortured. The contrast between the fresh hope of the young girl on the left and the fatalist resignation of her worldly wise self on the right, viewing the interlocked couple with an experienced disgust, is echoed in the harsh opposition of the red to the green and the black to the white.

The underlying sense of unease in this work pervades that of all members of the group. In Kirchner's *Artist and Model* (plate 21) the orange-blue dressing-gown strikes a harsh note, and the cautious apprehension of the model contributes to the calculated awkwardness of this extraordinarily rich painting. Schmidt-Rottluff's *Landscape* (plate 22) has the same rich heaviness of form and colour, and Nolde's *The Windmill* (plate 24) is laden with that air of remoteness and mystery which surrounds such romantic buildings. The sentimental romanticism of Pechstein's *Harbour* (plate 23), a particularly German characteristic, shows a tortured emotionalism which the somewhat contrived blue-orange complementary opposition aggravates. There is nothing in this work of the delicacy of French Fauvism.

The Blue Rider group is closely identified with Kandinsky and Marc, and the Expressionist nature of their work tends to more abstraction in form and colour. Beginning later than the Bridge group, the Blue Riders had a close contact with the contemporary movements in France, particularly with Cubism. The most important document of the group and one of the significant and essential writings by a painter in this century is Kandinsky's *Concerning the Spiritual in Art*, written in 1910 and published in 1912. Kandinsky came from Russia and brought with him, as did his compatriot Jawlensky, something of the mystical spirituality at the heart of the nation. He found in the deep natural sympathy of Marc a strong affinity. With the vitality of Jawlensky and the sensitive acuteness of Gabriele Munter, they explored together the possibilities of abstraction as a means of expressing their response to nature. Kandinsky has described his first experience of the abstract in some detail. Particularly revealing is the following incident described by Professor Grohmann: 'One day at twilight, he came into his studio and suddenly saw an "indescribably beautiful painting, permeated by an inner glow". He saw in it nothing but forms, no subject-matter at all. It was a picture he seemed to have made. The next day the spell was gone and he recognised the objects represented in it with painful distinctness. "Now I knew with certainty that the object harms my paintings." He had regarded the object as indispensable but now he realised the "ends (and hence also the means) of nature and art differ essentially, organically and by virtue of a universal law." ' Henceforward, the question for Kandinsky could not be 'what does it mean' in the aspect of logical or intellectual progression but what does it do in perceptual experience to my physiological and physical make-up — in other words, what aspect of the spirit does it touch? One can observe the distinction and development between the *Arab Cemetery* (plate 25) and *Black Lines* (plate 26). In the first the original natural forms can be seen extended and distorted towards the freer pattern of abstraction; in the latter the reference to any natural form has disappeared and the relationship of shapes, the colour and the web of black lines are the only means. Out of these springs a sense of gaiety and growth, of energy and movement.

Marc did not arrive at the complete abstraction of Kandinsky. His work always has a natural reference and in one of the most obviously abstract, *Fighting Forms* (plate 28) there is still a sense of large animals — a constant interest of Marc — locked in mortal combat, the colours and forms combining to give an overpowering sense of nature red in tooth and claw. The colour here is particularly interesting in that it is a clear example of the 'expressionist' use of colour relationships. Red energy opposes black defence which in its edges reveals the damage and despair it suffers.

The influence of Cubism is seen in the work of Feininger. In *The Square* (plate 31), however, the use of Cubism has not resulted in the fragmentation of the object as it has in, for instance, Braque's *The Portuguese* (plate 14) which points to the difference in intention. Colour in Feininger is used with an emotional intention, in this case to lend a gloomy dominance to the ordered forms of architecture over those of the human.

In Klee's painting *Young Girl's Adventure* (plate 32), which contains elements of Surrealism, the abstraction is of a different order from that of Kandinsky. Klee, one of the great masters of modern art, is concerned to reincarnate experience in a visible form, which has resulted in the widening of the division between his own being and 'nature' and which gives him a conviction of 'under-existence', the idea of 'creation as a genesis beneath the surface of the work'. His paintings generally use recognisable forms but with what has sometimes been wrongly described as a childish disregard for real relationships. Klee is concerned with the expression in possible visible form of what exists but which requires the peculiar sensitivity of the artist to personify it, or to make visible its nature. His paintings have a life of their own, a valid life; they may be conversed with, they may speak, nudge, seduce you or demand that you take off your hat to them; as Klee used to say, 'Now it looks at me.'

A certain charm, more Russian than German, is found in Jawlensky, and in *Peonies* (plate 29) he shows also that somewhat remote hieratic character which is a feature of his work.

A deep, passionate response to life and nature is a characteristic of German Expressionism, and this is nowhere better revealed than in the work of the independent Expressionists, Beckmann and Kokoschka. Beckmann's experience as a soldier during the First World War left him a legacy of depressed resentment at the brutality of man, at the debasement of ordinary life, at the amorality of woman. He searched his own face with an uncompromising directness — as if he carried in himself all the features of society which most disturbed him (plate 33). In *The Tempest* (plate 30) Kokoschka reveals a different spirit. Born in Austria and wounded in the First World War, he has been a permanent refugee from settled existence and has responded with a fierce ardour to the various places he has visited and the people he has met. He has managed to infuse an allegorical atmosphere even into his landscapes, and in *The Tempest* the two lovers are an allegory; for the interlocked forces of nature, of the fierce power of love and perhaps even of its poetry. In this painting, indeed, we see most of the characteristics that we have distinguished as Expressionist: power, emotional intensity, something of the mystic, not reflective but aggressive and immediate, not insinuating but attacking.

FUTURISM

The artists

Umberto Boccioni 1882—1916
Gino Severini 1883—1966
Carlo Carrà 1881—
Luigi Russolo 1885—1947
Giacomo Balla 1871—1958
Marcel Duchamp 1887—
Sant'Elia 1888—1916

In common with most modern art movements Futurism attracted a large number of followers in later years, but only the originators are listed above. Of these Boccioni was the driving force and apologist, whilst Severini has been perhaps the best known. Duchamp was not closely associated with the others but in some of his work he uses the principles of Futurism with more understanding and imagination than its originators. Sant'Elia was an architect and theoretician.

Pictorial characteristics

Futurist paintings are recognised by the characteristic division of the subject into a number of different positions which are all related together in one painting. This means that the paintings are not realist or straightforward, but are broken into areas and lines which interlock. The technique, which derives in part from Cubism, sometimes bears a close resemblance to it. Colour used by the Futurists varies from the Cubist browns and greens to the neo-pointillist colour in large dots of strong hue.

The name

The first use of the name Futurism in reference to art occurs in the Paris newspaper *Le Figaro* of 20th February 1909. In this issue the Italian poet Filippo Marinetti contributed the first 'Futurist Manifesto', a document of considerable interest and importance. Futurism is thus essentially an Italian art movement which resulted from the meeting in 1910 in Milan between Marinetti and the painters Boccioni, Carrà and Russolo. Marinetti inspired them to issue a 'Futurist Painters' Manifesto'. So, the name of this movement was chosen by the artists themselves and not attached to it, as with Fauvism and Cubism. Because of this the name might be supposed to be more relevant to the art of the group and, in so far as they are forward-looking and attempted to produce an art that would have importance for the future, this was so. The actual form that this art took is not so obviously related to the name — hardly surprising since each artist would have his own notion of the art of the future.

The origins and development

Filippo Marinetti (1876—1944), an Italian poet born in Egypt and educated in Paris, was the sponsor of Futurism as an intellectual movement. His essay in *Le Figaro* in 1909 extolled the beauty of speed, the virility of the new machine, the possibilities of the new scientific age — a new dynamic humanism. After a violently imaginative treatment of the emotional effect of speed in a motor car — Marinetti had a 60 h.p. Fiat — the manifesto lists what the Futurists felt and what they wished to do about the new century, changing conditions and expanding beliefs:

1. We will sing of the love of danger, the habits of energy and temerity.
2. Courage, audacity, revolt shall be the essential elements of our poetry.
3. Right down to the present, poetry has exalted moody immobility, ecstasy and repose. We shall exalt aggressive movement, feverish insomnia, life at the double, with somersaults, slaps and punches.

4. We assert that the magnificence of the world has been enriched by a new beauty, the beauty of speed. A racing car with its bonnet draped in enormous pipes like fire-spitting serpents . . . a roaring racing car that goes like a machine gun is more beautiful than the Winged Victory of Samothrace.

5. We will hymn the man at the wheel, whose ideal axis passes through the centre of the world, that is itself in full flight on the circuit of its orbit.

6. The poet must expend himself with ardour, ostentation and generosity to excite the fervour of all primitive elements.

7. There can be no beauty save in struggle. No work that lacks aggressive character can be a masterpiece. Poetry must be conceived as an assault on unknown powers, to make them bow down before man.

8. We are on the highest promontory of the centuries — why must we look back when we are about to break through the mysterious gates of the impossible. We live already in the absolute, since we have created universal eternal velocity.

9. We will glorify war, the only hygiene of the world — militarism, patriotism, the destructive gestures of anarchists, the great concepts of which men die, contempt of women.

10. We will destroy the museums, libraries and academies of every kind, and will combat moralism, feminism and all vile opportunist utilitarianism.

Such violent polemics could not fail to attract fanatical adherents, and wild irresponsibility succeeded the first attack on accepted standards. Later on the glorification of war and patriotism in Futurism was used by the Fascists and this at least partly accounts for a distaste which has led to the obscurity and lack of appreciation of Futurism in other countries.

Its effect was immediate and seemed to presage a new art. Soon a second manifesto followed and the movement was born. At this time the painters were only aware of the neo-Impressionist techniques and in 1911 they visited Paris with the intention of arranging an exhibition. They were dissuaded from this but while they were there they were introduced to the Cubist work of Picasso and Braque which by that time was becoming the *avant-garde* rage. Marcel Duchamp and Piet Mondrian were also in Paris at this time and Duchamp participated in the new art as it developed. The effect of this visit and the acquaintance with Cubism was to provide the Futurists, and particularly Boccioni and Carrà, with a new technique which they thought adaptable to their needs. The result was a sort of dynamic Cubism.

The projected Paris exhibition of Futurist work was held in the following year (1912) and this introduced the group and its ideas to a cosmopolitan European audience, thus widening its influence and finding new adherents. It still remained, however, essentially an Italian inspiration, and any attempt to internationalise it was resisted by Marinetti.

By the end of the First World War the urgency and excitement of the movement had evaporated partly because Boccioni, its chief polemicist and the most talented, had been killed in 1916. In any event, most of the original group had moved away from Futurism by 1918.

The nature of Futurism

The original manifesto quoted above indicates the character and intention of Futurist art. First, it was destructive: it believed that the changes brought by the new century and particularly its machine age character necessitated an art that reflected this and did not look back to the past. So strongly did they feel the danger of the past that the Futurists advocated the destruction of the monuments of the past, museums, art galleries and libraries — iconoclasm on the grand scale.

On the other hand, Futurism was aggressively constructive. It thought that an art could and should be built on the machine and its most obvious manifestation, speed. Movement, particularly mechanical sequential movement, seemed to them a typical and significant feature of this new age. They also associated the machine with masculinity — the assertive, active principle as opposed to the feminine, passive, acceptive principle.

Although each artist produced work that is distinct and personal, general Futurist characteristics may be observed which flow from this attitude. Concerned with movement, they attempted to present it in sequential form and arrived at paintings in which the movement of figure or machine is expressed by painting the moving object in several successive positions in the same painting; thus a figure may have a number of legs and arms as in Severini's *Dynamic Hieroglyphic of the Bal Tabarin* (plate 39), or a machine may be shown as a series of interlocking wheels. Interested in the dynamic of modern life, they sought to find it in series of overlapping, integrated, progressional forms. Marcel Duchamp's *Nude Descending a Staircase* (plate 18) is an example of this sequential movement and Duchamp has himself explained the picture. 'It is an organisation of kinetic elements, an expression of time and space through the abstract presentation of motion. A painting is, of necessity, a juxtaposition of two or more colours on a surface. I purposely restricted the *Nude* to wood colouring so that the question of painting *per se* might not be raised. There are, I admit, many patterns by which this idea could be expressed. Art would be a poor muse if there were not. But remember, when we consider the motion of form through space in a given time, we enter the realm of geometry and mathematics, just as we do when we build a machine for that purpose. Now if I show the ascent of an aeroplane, I try to show what it does. I do not make a still life picture of it. When the vision of the *Nude* flashed upon me, I knew that it would break for ever the enslaving chains of Naturalism.'

The Balla *Dog on a Leash* (plate 38) is a painting of a different order and throws up another aspect of Italian Futurism — its pictorial naivety. Although the intention is to present action in sequence, the vision is essentially naturalistic and hampered by Balla's inability to create a real sequential expression. In the painting the body is realised in one spot and only the numerous legs give the sense of motion in the animal, while the ground is presented as passing — as in a film in which the camera focuses on a galloping horse, and the ground dissolves into lines of movement. The movement of the body and its progress in space and time are not considered. Such pictorial simplicity is endearing and humorous but barely exploratory. The painting methods adopted by the Futurists varied from a neo-Impressionist 'pointillisme' to a Cubist build up of planes and facets. In the three examples of Boccioni's painting illustrated his development towards the later form indicating sequential movement is revealed.

The City Rises (plate 34) is a set piece of neo-Impressionist emotionalism. The rushing urgent activity of the early day and its uncomprehending irresistible face are symbolised in the dissolving forms of the horses and the tensed stretched workmen. It is a strange work in which Boccioni is obviously still trying to find a satisfactory expression of movement. In the later painting *Elasticity* (plate 35) again the horse appears, though some of the urgent force is replaced by a decorative interlocking of shapes derived from the movement of the animal and rider. In this painting Boccioni begins to find some of the spiky, swirling forms he uses again later.

In *The Charge of the Lancers* (plate 36), painted after the outbreak of war, some of the energy and urgency has returned; the colour has become more sombre, a mechanical power is introduced. Again one sees the horse but this time it is representative of force itself, dangerous but exciting. It is perhaps as well to recall that Boccioni was killed in the following year as the result of a fall from a horse.

A more sophisticated example of Balla's Futurism than his *Dog on a Leash* is his *Speeding Automobile* (plate 37) where he has tried to express in an abstract interlocking of forms the fascination of the new power of the car that held all Futurists.

In the *Houses and Lights* (plate 40) by Russolo we have a

reflection of the mechanical repetition of events found in a great city.

The justification for this work, as with so much of the early work of the century, lies more in the attitude and fresh intention than in the achievement of the individual paintings. Boccioni's first manifesto sums up their attitude:

That all forms of imitation should be held in contempt and that all forms of originality should be glorified.

That we should rebel against the tyranny of the words 'harmony' and 'good taste'. With these expressions, which are too elastic, it would be possible to demolish the works of Rembrandt, Goya and Rodin.

That sincerity and virginity more than any other qualities are necessary to the interpretation of nature.

That motion and light destroy the materiality of bodies.

Like Fauvism and Cubism, Futurism was a movement of young enthusiastic men, who were impatient of reflection, volatile, voluble and Latin in temperament. In Futurism we have the first conscious attempt to create an art which derived its forms and its attitude from the twentieth century. It essayed prophesy in that it forecast the dominance of speed in modern life and saw the beginning of the decay of classical standards. Surrounded by the nostalgic reverence for the Renaissance and confronted with its relics on all sides, it is hardly surprising that in their urgent energy the Futurists were impatient of the passive acceptance of earlier standards. Like most revolutionaries they used inflated language in their writing but they were sincere reformers.

It is unfortunate perhaps that, with the single exception of Boccioni, they were not greatly talented and failed to develop a consistent or effective form for their ideas. That they so quickly deserted the movement after the death of Boccioni suggests that they themselves realised the pictorial inadequacy of their Futurist work.

Futurism is predominantly a painting movement but before leaving it the sculptures of Boccioni should be mentioned. Posterity may well consider that it is in this work of Boccioni's that the most important examples of Futurism are to be found, and it is certainly true that Boccioni is one of the significant sculptors of the century; his *Unique Forms of Continuity in Space* is a modern masterpiece.

The influence of Futurism may also be seen in the drawings of cities of the future by the Italian architect Sant'Elia in which the uninterrupted horizontal and vertical flow of traffic and the open planning are extraordinarily visionary.

DE STIJL

The artists

Theo van Doesburg (C.E.M. Küpper) 1883—1931
Piet Mondrian 1872—1944
Bart van der Leck 1876—1958
Georges Vantongerloo 1886—1965
J.J.P. Oud 1890—1963
Gerit Rietveld 1888—1964
Cornelis van Eesteren 1897—
Constantin Brancusi 1876—1957
Jans Wils 1891—
Cesar Domela 1900—
Hans Richter 1888—
Vilmos Huszar 1884—1960
El Lissitsky 1890—1941

This group comprised painters, sculptors, architects, designers and illustrators and the above list contains some of each, though only paintings are illustrated. The most typical figures in the group are Van Doesburg and Mondrian in that the former was the creator and inspiration and the latter the best-known member.

Pictorial characteristics

The most uncompromisingly abstract of all modern painting, De Stijl work can be recognised by the use of the primary colours (red, yellow and blue) or near primaries, and horizontal and vertical lines dividing the areas of the canvas. In one characteristic of De Stijl, the vertical and horizontal lines give way to diagonals but the same use of primaries is observed.

The name

De Stijl is Dutch for 'The Style'. It was the name given by Van Doesburg to the periodical of the arts that he first produced in 1917. The introduction to the first issue contains the following: 'The object of this little periodical is to contribute something towards a new sense of beauty. It wishes to make the modern man aware of the new ideas that have sprung up in the plastic arts. It wants to set up the logical principles of a maturing style which is based upon a clearer relation between the spirit of the age and the means of expression, against the archaic confusion, the "modern baroque". It wants to combine in itself the present day ideas on modern plastic art, ideas which, though fundamentally the same, have been developed individually and independently...'

Without describing the particular form the art of the group took, this passage shows that its intention was similar to other modern movements in its dissatisfaction with the existing situation and in its determination to produce a new relevant art.

Neo Plasticism was the term Mondrian preferred to De Stijl as descriptive of the movement. Mondrian said that Neo Plasticism was the means by which the variety and ingenuity of nature could be reduced to a plastic configuration defining natural relationships. Thus art could become the method of communicating the immanent order of nature.

The origins and development

The name of the group, De Stijl, indicates its Dutch origin. It is the Dutch contribution to the development of modern art and in Mondrian it has one of the most uncompromising of modern painters.

The movement has received less general attention than the other groups considered here, partly because it has appeared to be so uncompromisingly 'abstract', partly because by the time it had formed Paris had become the recognised and apparently only centre of creative experiment, partly because since the seventeenth-century Holland had not been looked to for creative work, and partly because the group was never stable, members joining, resigning or just sliding away at all times after 1917.

The only continuous apologist and enthusiast was Van Doesburg whose inspiration the whole movement was. He has said: '... the embryo of what was realised five years later, in the idea and the periodical *De Stijl*, was at the base of the thought I had formulated in 1912; strip nature of its forms and you will have style left.' Throughout his life Van Doesburg worked energetically for the group and its ideas; he was the core and centre of its activities. When he died in 1931 the group ceased to exist, although the ideas which it had formulated had in any case become part of the whole modern idea of pictorial expression.

Curiously, however, De Stijl is generally associated more with the painter Mondrian than with Van Doesburg. Mondrian's theory of Neo Plasticism is essentially different from Van Doesburg's, and so much did they disagree that in 1925 Mondrian left De Stijl.

Although, as Van Doesburg indicated in the passage quoted above, discussion which led to De Stijl started as early as 1912, the public inauguration of the movement did not occur until 1917 with the publication of the periodical *De Stijl*. The editor and principal contributor was Van Doesburg (he also used two other pen-names, Bonset and Camini; his real name, Küpper, he never used). Other contributors were Mondrian, Van der Leck and Huszar. Apart from this literary beginning, the group was also working in architecture (J.J.P. Oud built two important houses at this time) and furniture (Rietveld was the designer).

In the following year the group published its first manifesto. It begins as follows: 'There is an old and a new consciousness of time. The old is connected with the individual. The new is connected with the universal. The struggle of the individual against the universal is revealing itself in the world war as well as in the art of the present day.' One is reminded here of the whole classic attitude, of order and organisation.

The manifesto was intended as a call to other artists outside Holland, and after the Armistice of 1918 they responded. French, Italian, Belgian and German artists began to contribute to the magazine.

In 1920 Mondrian published his pamphlet *Neo Plasticism* in Paris, where he was at that time working, and an essay in the form of a dialogue, *Natural Reality and Abstract Reality*. Both these difficult documents are explanations of Mondrian's attitude. In 1921 the centre of De Stijl activity was in Germany where Van Doesburg had made contact with Walter Gropius, the recently appointed head of the Bauhaus at Weimar. Van Doesburg had visions of converting this famous design school to his ideas and for a short while he was a member of the staff but his energies could not be confined in this way. Of the period he says, 'At Weimar I have radically overturned everything. This is the famous academy, which now had the most modern teachers. I have talked to the pupils every evening and have infused the poison of the new spirit everywhere.' During the next three years the centre shifted from Germany to Paris and a number of architectural works were designed which, as Van Doesburg claimed in 1924, broke new ground. 'The house has been analysed; it has been dissected into its plastic elements. The static axis of the old construction has been destroyed. The house has become an object; one can circle it on all sides. This analytical method led to new possibilities of construction and to a new ground plan.' One has only to travel in Holland now to see the impact of these ideas. In 1923 the first house to incorporate them completely was designed and built by Rietveld.

In 1925 the differences between Van Doesburg and Mondrian led to the latter leaving the movement. The basis of the disagreement is of some importance in the understanding of the movement and is discussed later. The effect was to throw even more responsibility on Van Doesburg, to split the movement and to deprive it of its most creative artist. Van Doesburg developed a new theory which he called 'Elementarism', and this became the characteristic of the group. It happened that Van Doesburg soon after received a commission to restyle the interior of the Aubette at Strasbourg and he was able to make this a public expression of Elementarism. The mural in the cinema dance hall was the most striking part.

After Strasbourg Van Doesburg returned to Paris where he intended to open a design school and prepared a studio at Meudon. Before it was completed he died at Davos where he had been taken to recuperate from a serious illness. With him De Stijl died; he was the only one who knew all the members personally and kept the group together. Although the members went their separate ways, the architects, some of whom were in influential positions, continued to propagate in their work the ideas of De Stijl. Van Eesteren became the Chief Engineer and city planner to Amsterdam in 1929, J.J.P. Oud became City Architect to Rotterdam in 1918, Rietveld designed the Netherlands Pavilion at the Venice Biennale in 1953, and Jan Wils designed the Olympic Stadium in Amsterdam in 1928.

Mondrian, after leaving the movement, remained in Paris until 1938 when he came to England where he was bombed out in 1940. Thereafter he lived in New York until his death in 1944.

Van Doesburg and Mondrian both had a following in America which has had some influence on recent American developments. In Europe Cesar Domela has been a follower of Van Doesburg's Elementarism.

The nature of De Stijl and Neo Plasticism

Initially at least, these two terms may be considered together, Neo Plasticism being preferred by Mondrian to describe his work, while De Stijl describes the group.

Of all modern movements this is the one which probably proves the most difficult of comprehension to the widest section of the public and which is for them the least attractive. The reason is not, I think, far to seek. In the Introduction we have discussed in general terms the nature and purpose of abstraction and have noticed it as a recurring tendency of modern art. Indeed, we have used a development of abstraction by Mondrian to illustrate the progressive stages in the process. In most cases, including the Mondrian series, the quality of abstraction is one of degree from some natural form — which is often distinguishable, as in most Cubist examples (see plates 11, 14).

This is not true of the mature De Stijl work which arrives at its abstract form not by a process of removes from a given subject but from an intellectual idea of the attainability of the expression of universal order, that order being immanent in nature. De Stijl artists were thus not concerned with the incidental aspects of nature or with the individual interpretation of them. Mondrian has written:

Man is enabled by abstract aesthetic contemplation to achieve conscious unity with the universal.

The deepest purpose in painting has always been to give concrete existence, through line and colour, to the universal which appears in contemplation.

Real life is the mutual interaction of two oppositions of the same value but of a different aspect and nature. Its plastic expression is universal beauty.

Cesar Domela, in a lecture about abstract art and De Stijl, says:

Lines, surfaces and colours are units with which the artist creates forces that enable him to organise the picture. For these forces to achieve their maximum intensity, it is necessary to simplify forms. The composition forms a whole and nothing can be added or taken away from it. Colour is used for its dynamic effect and not for its prettiness.

And Mondrian again:

Unconsciously every true artist has always been moved by beauty of line, colour and relationship for their own sake and not by what they may represent.

Abstract-real painting is capable of mathematically aesthetic expression, because it possesses an exact, mathematical means of expression. This means of expression is definitely established colour. The definite establishment of colour implies: 1. the reduction of natural colour to primary colour; 2. the reduction of colour to flatness; 3. the enclosure of colour, so that it appears as a unity of rectangular planes.

These quotations give some idea of the intentions of De Stijl. It was to produce an art of autonomous beauty, independent of individuality, with the simplest elements, an art which, as Domela has put it, would be grasped as readily in Stockholm as in Athens — that is, with no local limitations, no temperamental exclusions.

These ideas of abstraction were, of course, in the air at this time and the influence of Cubism is obvious; we shall see it in the work of Mondrian when we examine the plates. The influence upon Mondrian of the Dutch mathematician and philosopher M.H.J. Shoenmakers must, however, be mentioned, for most of the beliefs he held appear to have come from Shoenmaker's writings and from numerous conversations between the two. It is also obviously of significance that one of Shoenmakers's books is entitled *Principles of Plastic Mathematics* which he explains: 'Plastic mathematics means true and methodical thinking from the point of view of the creator.' It was from the philosopher, too, that Mondrian took his artistic equations of line: vertical — male — space — statics — harmony; horizontal — female — time — dynamic — melody.

The deliberate attempt at the exclusion of individuality, personality and temperament should be noticed. Van Doesburg once asserted, 'I abhor all that is temperament, inspiration, sacred fire and all the attributes of genius that conceal the untidiness of the mind.' A little surprising from Van Doesburg, perhaps, since temperament and inspiration seem the characteristics he most exhibited and one might also say that there is a good deal of evidence of the 'sacred fire' in Mondrian.

A distinction between principles and practice, or at least a difficulty in equating the two, is a troublesome feature of the art of De Stijl. Part of the difficulty no doubt arises from the simplicity of the means: Mondrian, as in his *Composition* (plate 42), uses vertical and horizontal black lines and the primary colours; with Van Doesburg (plate 44) and Domela (plate 46), diagonal lines and the primary colours. The diagonals represent the development of Elementarism to which Mondrian took so much exception, feeling it to be too idiosyncratic.

No art previously had so limited itself as did De Stijl to such austere means, and it is quite remarkable how effective they can be in the work of Mondrian. His progress to his mature art is indicated in the illustrations. The pictures in the Introduction show the first stages in his move towards abstraction and indicate, too, the preoccupation that we have noted in connection with the modern movements with the canvas' surface. Figure 3 (frontispiece) is Cubist, built of planes lying across the surface. In *Composition* (plate 41) Mondrian has not arrived at a simplicity or integration in his forms; he is not using the primary colours, and the proportions of the canvas are indeterminate. At the same time the painting is abstract, concerned only with relationships of areas of colour and a broken black grid which floats over and pinions the colour areas to the space surrounding them. This is not a deep expression of natural relationships; it is a stage in Mondrian's progress and shows how he is trying to find elements which will combine to his purpose. It is clear that there is a close relationship between this painting and Van der Leck's (plate 45) although one notices that Leck is using the primary colours at this time. A comparison of the two paintings is interesting. The disposition of these simple, similar elements in similarly proportioned canvases produces different paintings, not merely in the arrangement but in the feeling. There is a quiet calm harmony in the Mondrian and a more aggressive, mechanical, active quality in the Van der Leck. In Mondrian there is no repetition, only balance; in the Van der Leck the action depends on repetition and counterpoint. Thus will temperaments always express themselves.

Van Doesburg's *Counter Composition* (plate 44) and Mondrian's *Composition* (plate 42) show the character of mature De Stijl. Van Doesburg's painting is an example of Elementarism which attempted to introduce a more varied form of expression, deliberately unstable with inclined planes, which Van Doesburg felt went beyond the limited Neo Plasticism of Mondrian. Mondrian's painting here illustrated is a very good example of his mature work. The elements are vertical and horizontal lines and the primary colours, and it is only in the balance of their relationships that the painting can act. As Mondrian said in the dedication, to Professor Alfred Roth, of his *Composition*, 'to reckon only with relationships by creating them and by seeking a balance between them in art and in life — this is the fine work for today and a preparation for the future.' The picture is divorced from natural appearance, and the canvas is square. The effect of the large area of red, which makes the initial impact, is not to swamp the blue and yellow but to give them value, so that the eye moves from the red across the black step to the blue and accepts the yellow reference in its return to the demanding red. Such is the balance that an indefinable statement — that is indefinable in words — is made which leaves one with the feeling that one's understanding of relationships, of intensities, of properties has been enlarged. If this sounds unconvincing, destroy the balance by removing one element.

In *Broadway Boogie Woogie* (plate 43) the later Mondrian, influenced by the American scene, appears. Without forsaking the vertical and horizontal or the primaries, Mondrian is here suggesting the range and variety, the excited mechanism of American life — the dancing steps of the 'asphalt jungle' — as well as revealing his own inherent romanticism.

A comparison between the mature Mondrian (plate 42) and the Domela (plate 46) is interesting. Though the pictures are of apparently similar means and similar in balance, the single effect of diagonal emphasis in the Domela creates a more dynamic aggressive character and really distinguishes the different temperaments.

The influence of De Stijl has, of course, been considerable — in commercial design of all forms and in architecture. In architecture it has been through the work of the De Stijl architects rather than through the work of the painters, although in the attempt to express internal volumes and to interrelate areas of space the work of Mondrian is an important stimulus. At one time Mies Van der Rohe was associated with De Stijl.

SURREALISM

The artists

Max Ernst 1891—

Salvador Dali 1904—

Giorgio di Chirico 1888—

Joan Miró 1893—

Yves Tanguy 1900—1955

René Magritte 1898—

Jean Arp 1887—1966

Francis Picabia 1878—1953

Kurt Schwitters 1887—1948

Paul Klee 1879—1940

Man Ray 1890—

Marc Chagall 1887—

Marcel Duchamp 1887—

Surrealism is a very adaptable name and is used to describe a great variety of work, from the pure fantasy to the involved allegory or dream image. In consequence the number of artists whose names could be listed is extensive. The above artists perhaps indicate both the range and main characteristics of the movement in its earlier period.

Pictorial characteristics

Dealing with the fantastic, Surrealist painting may take a number of distinct forms, each of which, however, is recognisable through the irrational approach and the construction of unreal, unworldly, mysterious figures, either painted extremely meticulously, or constructed in near abstract shapes.

The name

Surrealism is divided into two periods of development, the earlier pre-Surrealist phase being known by the name of Dada.

Dada was the name adopted by a group of writers and painters who were in Zürich in 1915. They were disillusioned refugees who saw in the war the destruction of society, loss of purpose and a pessimistic future. The name was chosen at random from a German-French dictionary (it means 'hobby-horse') as a deliberate way of expressing the inconsequential, irrational character of the group's intentions.

Surrealism was a word used by Apollinaire to describe a play he wrote in 1917 (*drame surréaliste en deux actes et un prologue*) which was adopted by André Breton, the chief apologist and guiding spirit of Surrealism. Surrealism was defined by Breton, as he said, 'once for all time':

Surrealism, n. Pure psychic automatism, by which it is intended to express, whether verbally or in writing, or in any other way, the real process of thought. Thought's dictation, free from any control by the reason, independent of any aesthetic or moral preoccupation.

Encycl. *Philos.* Surrealism rests on the belief in the superior reality of certain forms of association hitherto neglected, in the omnipotence of the dream, in the disinterested play of thought. It tends definitely to destroy all other mechanisms and to substitute itself for them in the solution of the principal problems of life.

This is from the *First Surrealist Manifesto* written by André Breton and published in 1924.

No more accurate than the names attached to other groups, Surrealism as a term nevertheless gives some idea of the art associated with it. Above the real, super real — it is the art of the fantastic, of the subconscious, of dream.

The origins and development

En Avant Dada; a History of Dadaism was published in 1920 by Richard Hülsenbeck, one of its original members. He explains that 'Dada was founded in Zürich in the spring of 1916 by Hugo Ball, Tristan Tzara, Jean Arp, Marcel Janko and Richard Hülsenbeck at the Cabaret Voltaire, a little bar where Hugo Ball and his friend Emmy Hennings had set up a miniature variety show, in which all of us were very active.'

Zürich, a neutral city, became a refuge for artists and a close association developed between writers and artists who were dismayed and disillusioned by the war. The group expressed their feelings in a number of publications, experimental films, constructions and paintings. The centre of their operations and, incidentally, the name they gave their publication, was the Cabaret Voltaire mentioned by Hülsenbeck. This was a form of arts club with a stage and an exhibition and lecture hall. The entertainments they provided give some idea of the wild irresponsibility and destructive zeal of its members. These were deliberately designed to outrage the mystified public who were nevertheless attracted by the strange scene. In weird costumes reciting nonsense poems to the sound of gongs, rattles, and tubes of brass beaten with hammers, the Dadaists postured obscenely. Almost simultaneously similar manifestations appeared throughout Europe and America and most notably in Paris and New York. Paris became at last the centre of the Dada activities, and encouraged by public attacks and incomprehension it went from excess to excess until in 1922 it was succeeded by the formation of Surrealism proper. Although there are 'artistic' manifestations of Dada it was primarily a literary movement. Nevertheless in the collages by Jean Arp, the child machines working hard to no purpose by Francis Picabia and the objects, 'readymades', of Marcel Duchamp (not *Nude Descending Staircase* illustrated) Dada had created something of real shock value. The most famous, perhaps, of Marcel Duchamp's 'objects' is the reproduction of the *Mona Lisa* on which he had chalked a moustache with the obscene caption 'LHOOQ' — a deliberate gesture against the art of the museums.

André Breton, the apologist for Surrealism, came to believe that Dada was nothing more than 'a rough image of a state of mind which it by no means helped to create' and became increasingly unsympathetic towards the irrational and puerile antics of the Dadaists who wanted nothing of art. He felt that some positive creative activity, the result of intellectual analysis of the modern age, should be engaged in. The result was Surrealism which drew inspiration from a number of sources but particularly from the psychoanalysts. Breton, as a medical student, had come into contact with the writings of Freud. In 1924 Breton published the *First Surrealist Manifesto* which he followed in 1929 with a second. During the twenties and thirties the influence of Breton and his writings extended widely through Europe and America and Surrealism expressed itself in a number of different forms. Poetry, literature, films, music as well as painting all produced examples. Particularly interesting are two films made by Luis Buñuel, *Le chien andalou* (1929) and *L'âge d'or* (1931) which are entirely Surrealist in character and perhaps the most enduring examples of its shock technique.

Throughout the thirties most countries held exhibitions of Surrealist work and almost invariably these were accompanied by incomprehension and vilification in the popular press. Surrealism became at this time the term frequently used to encase all modern painting, however remote from it, and it has since held a certain currency as synonymous with all modern art. There was a small support for the Surrealists among the intellectuals and *cognoscenti* in each country in which they appeared but mystification was the common response. For example, every national newspaper condemned the International Surrealist Exhibition which opened in June 1936 in London, the *Daily Express* saying that it was unfit for the public at large. A certain section of intellectuals led by Mr Herbert (now Sir Herbert) Read and Mr Roland (now Sir Roland) Penrose, himself a Surrealist painter, supported the Surrealists. Sir Herbert Read in his introduction to a selection of Surrealist writing published at the time, wrote '. . . the International Surrealist Exhibition broke over London electrifying the dry intellectual atmosphere, stirring our sluggish minds to wonder, enchantment and derision. The press, unable to appreciate the significance of a movement of such unfamiliar features, prepared an armoury of mockery, sneers and insults. The duller desiccated weeklies, no less impelled to anticipate the event, commissioned their polyglot gossips, their blasé globe trotters, their old boy scouts, to adopt their usual pose of "I know all, don't be taken in, there is nothing new under the sun" — a pose which merely reflects the general lack of intellectual curiosity in the country.' This passage, as well as accurately estimating the situation, reflects something of indignant shock that the sensitive spirits received from Surrealism. They were jolted into self-analysis and awareness — which, as we shall see later, was a deliberate and important part of the intention of the Surrealists.

A similar public attitude to that outlined above is found in all the other countries in which Surrealism manifested itself. As time passed, however, two main courses of development appeared. At the same time the formerly outrageous behaviour of the Surrealists became increasingly tolerated or pitied and this in turn dissuaded the Surrealists from such attacks on conventional attitudes and they increasingly confined themselves to producing work. This began, for obvious reasons, to partake more and more of the aspect of art — that is to say, as paintings or sculpture — and by the forties and noticeably since the war, Surrealists have appeared in group or mixed exhibitions with little consciousness of incongruity. Thus, Surrealism from being an anti-art iconoclastic movement, deliberately bent on the destruction of the whole conventional art world, has become an acceptable attitude, reflecting the fantastic and mystical and turning often to emotional pattern making.

The two main characteristics of later development are easily recognised. On the one hand there are the successors of the Dadaists who are still anti-art, nihilist and destructive, who have only to recognise a rule of art to wish to break it; on the other there is the Surrealist tradition of aesthetic construction, which although adhering to a different standard of beauty nevertheless had one and its followers were prepared to construct their work on its principles. It is, of course, this form that predominates at present.

The nature of Surrealism

Watches draped over withered tree stumps, animated but dismembered figures, dream evocation, unreasonable and often erotic association of objects in irrational scale, near abstract symbols of sexual reference — these are elements in the form of art that is known as Surrealism. For the majority of people such material is not proper to art, but it is the nature of Surrealism to introduce different subjects and some measure of its success that it has managed to achieve its acceptance. Part of the reason for this no doubt lies in the fascination that human nature seems to have for the turned-over stone, the weird, the half-realised, the dangerous, the unexpected and feared. It is attracted, even mesmerised, in a mood of cautious revulsion — and convention suggests it should not be interested and discourages acknowledgement of the desire.

Such distaste and fascination is Surrealist currency and the history of painting abounds in examples of this uncovering of the unconscious and the presentation of the visually impossible — or at least improbable — in the most visually convincing terms. Sometimes, as in the bestiaries of the Middle Ages, the monster figures stem from a real belief in the existence of the unseen super-real world and a conscious imaginative attempt to personify them. Later this is extended into an attempt to present a thesis in visual terms which its author is aware is not natural but which he feels to be true in essence — examples are found in the works of Breughel and Bosch. Here the allegory is a justification of the imagery. Sometimes flights of visual fancy have been responsible for a form of Surrealism — the vegetable men of Archimboldo, the incongruous contiguity of the inmates of the forests in Douanier Rousseau and even the 'grotesques' of Leonardo.

More powerful in recent Surrealism has been the impact of psycho-analysis and its revelation of the deep sexual responses in our human nature. The writings and case histories of Freud and his followers provided the Surrealists directly with the means of expression. They were aware of the importance of the analyst's enquiry and felt that it provided them with an opportunity to enlarge the language of art, particularly as they were becoming increasingly convinced that the art of the day was a dead restraint. The case histories also provided them with a method of shock treatment on the public mind. Overt sexuality and its art expression is a sure-fire public talking point and the early Surrealists used it extensively.

Another method adopted, almost as certain of success, was to ridicule the common artifacts of society by destroying their practical utility — hence the fur-lined teacup, saucer and spoon of Oppenheim, the *Cadeau* of Man Ray (a flat-iron on the base of which tacks had been attached) and Marcel Duchamp's *Fountain* (a gentlemen's urinal). A number of such common objects were included in Surrealist exhibitions and called by Duchamp 'ready-mades'.

As we have already noted the earliest manifestation of this attitude occurs in Dada. Dada everywhere was anti-art. It felt (one is always inclined to discuss Dada as a single entity although the individual irresponsibility of its members was central to its nature) that there was an essential irrelevance in the common aesthetic, which constructed its art from predigested standards of beauty, from a heritage of forms and methods of composition which are generally familiar and act as a substitute for the act of creation itself. It is a question of recognition; the packaged experience is bought unopened on its known label quality. Not only the Surrealists, but most of their creative contemporaries reacted against this, as they believed, induced pseudo-experience. They chose different methods and directions in avoiding the obvious and familiar and in their attempt at the enlargement of experience. The Surrealists were inspired with a desire to shock off the first conventional skin on the body aesthetic and prod the defence-less raw flesh uncovered below. To expand the metaphor, Dada was the irresponsible young surgeon who opened the body and skipped off leaving the raw wound whilst the Surrealist did the probing with at least some appearance of methodical care.

Within this context Surrealism has a wide scope. It is limited neither in method nor technique, and the range of expression is considerable: Max Ernst developed a technique (*frottage*) which, rather like brass rubbing, gave a curious, vague but emotional evocation of landscape or figure; Dali used a meticulously naturalistic technique in heavily con-structed irrationalities; Miró evolved an abstract sexual sym-bolism; Chirico invented a meditative dream world of eerie conviction — the list could be extended.

The selection we illustrate gives some indication of this variety. In Max Ernst's *Of This Men Shall Know Nothing* (plate 47) the sexuality is obvious and the symbolism precise. He has inscribed the back with this descriptive passage: 'The Crescent (yellow and parachutic) stops the little whistle falling to the ground. The whistle, because people are taking notice of it, thinks it is climbing to the sun. / The sun is divided in two so that it can spin better. / The model is stretched out in a dreaming pose. The right leg is bent (a pleasant, exact movement). / The hand hides the earth. Through this movement the earth takes on the importance of a sexual organ. / The moon runs through its phases and eclipses with the utmost speed. / The picture is curious because of its symmetry. The two sexes balance each other.' In the other painting, *Monument to Birds* (plate 48) Ernst's fascination for birds is expressed in a painting of brooding calm and dignity: in a deep open sky forms of carved pigeons float for ever, watching and cautious. This is the essence of the dream evocation.

In Dali's *Premonition of Civil War* (plate 49) the sensational exhibitionism of the painter's work, the sexuality, meticulous technique and unmemorable drawing are all in evidence. The symbolism is more private but the message is still clear. In Chirico's painting (plate 53) a quieter mystical spirit prevails. The long shadows and unreal light, the dreamlike colonnaded piazza, the classical figure sculpture evoke a calm which is menaced by the harsh suggestion of an industrial world behind the distant wall. This is an art of brooding unease and emotional fantasy. With Magritte's *Time Transfixed* (plate 51) all is reasonable except the one irrational object of the train appearing through the fireplace. The evocative effect of this will vary with each individual but in every case will be the result of the forced juxtaposition of two normally unassociated objects. This again is part of the nature of Surrealism.

The 'merz' painting by Schwitters (plate 52) is of another kind. Schwitters invented the term 'merz' to describe a form of collage made of rejected bric-à-brac which he thought could show that the usual materials of art are not necessary and that ordinary compositional standards need not apply. It was also another form of the protest against conventional attitudes that the Surrealists devised. Schwitters himself has inscribed the back of this work 'Merz ist nicht Dada', and said that he was antagonistic to the iconoclasm of Dada: he wished to construct a new image out of the bric-à-brac of useless material.

A comparison of the two paintings *Maternity* by Miró and Chagall (plates 50, 54) shows the possible range of Surrealist symbolism. In the Miró abstract forms have a very obvious sexual derivation and are like a pictorial diagram of the fertilisation process with magnified representation of sperm and ovum. The warmth and care of motherhood are absent. In Chagall the physical aspect of motherhood is presented with the child seen in the womb but there is also a rich symbolism of the life that the child is going to enter — mysterious and commonplace, full of labour but also of joy.

This wide range in Surrealism is its principle characteristic and is responsible for its continued appearance. At the same time the familiarity which, we are told, breeds contempt has begun to work against the effectiveness of the Surrealist pictorial idea. One shock to the system can be salutary — the constant application of similar shocks becomes tedious and boring. For this reason the Surrealists are constantly searching in their private world for new methods of attack to the extent that they are achieving variety without point.

Henri-Matisse

3

4

5

6

7

8

9

Collection, The Museum of Modern Art, New York

13

15

17

NU DESCENDANT UN ESCALIER MARCEL DUCHAMP

18

19

22

23

24

27

28

30

31

34

Collection, The Museum of Modern Art, New York

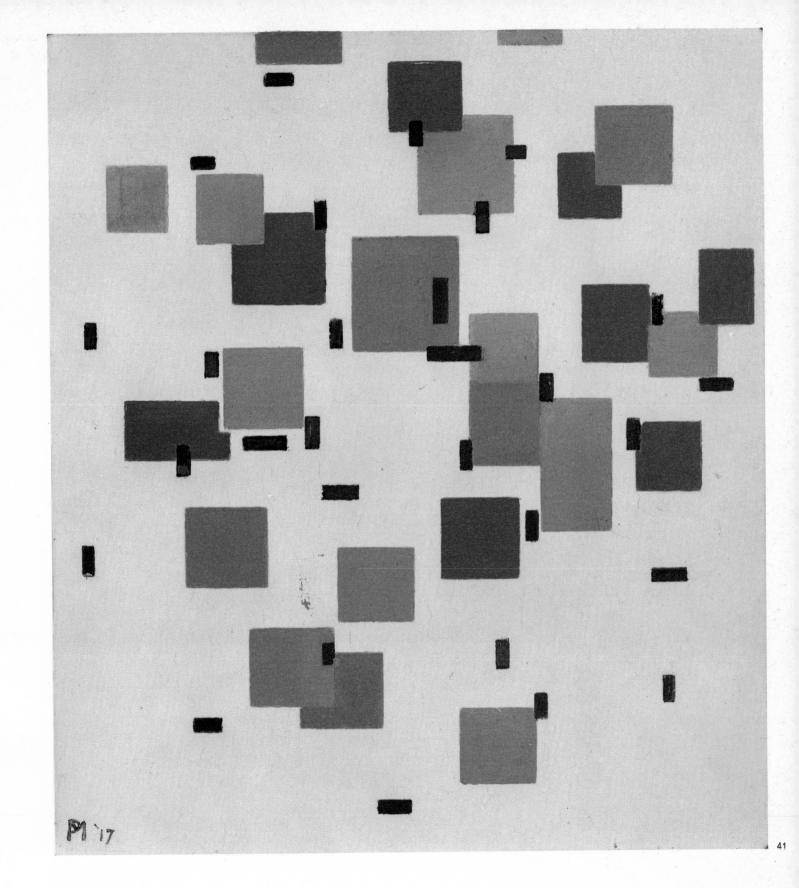

PM '17

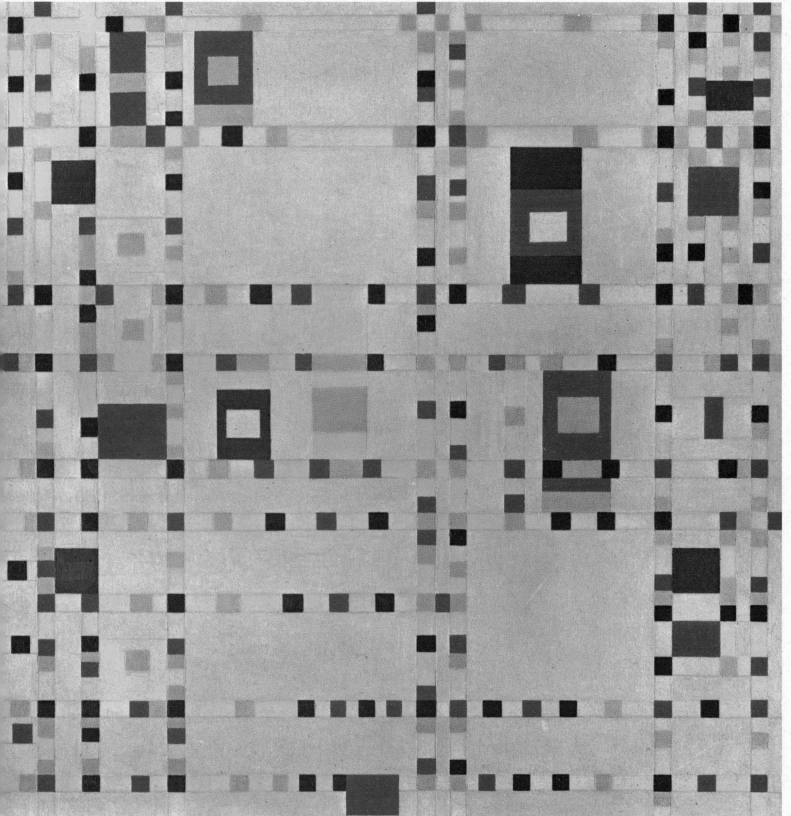

49

51

53